ARTEC Architekten

Bettina Götz + Richard Manahl

PARK BOOKS

I The ARTEC grammar

Fuzzy House
Cologne
1993

The idea was to employ a small number of large-format building components – like a house of cards – to give users a basic structure that they may appropriate and adapt to their needs.

Thus, on account of its properties, we chose to work with 3s – a multi-layer wood board. The 3s panel can be employed versatilely as structural member, and, thanks to its thickness, has insulting properties, but above all, is strong all over.

This board is the chip in the building complex, but its specific function as building component does not become apparent until it has been installed. Every wall is load-bearing and isolated per se. The board's dimensions are 2 × 6 meters at a thickness of 10 centimeters. The infill elements of the outer skin are translucent and fix mounted or operable; the technical fitting-out requires no shafts. The building becomes an autonomous device, as the installations – in both senses – are visible, graspable, and freely accessible from all points.

Because the terms *outside* and *inside* have been done away with, the layer that encloses space is no longer perceptible – or, in other words, is out of focus.

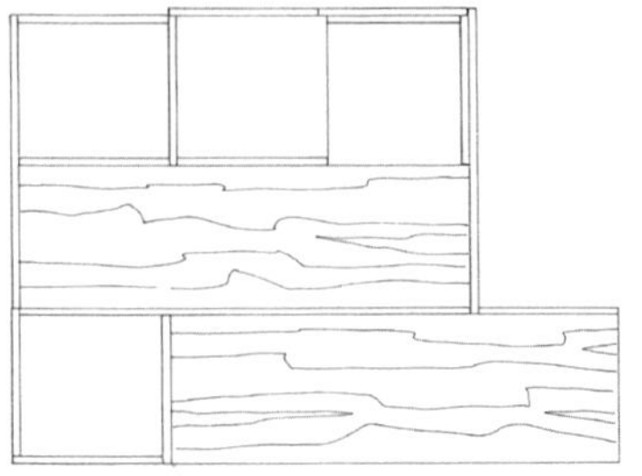

ANSICHT 1

ANSICHT 2

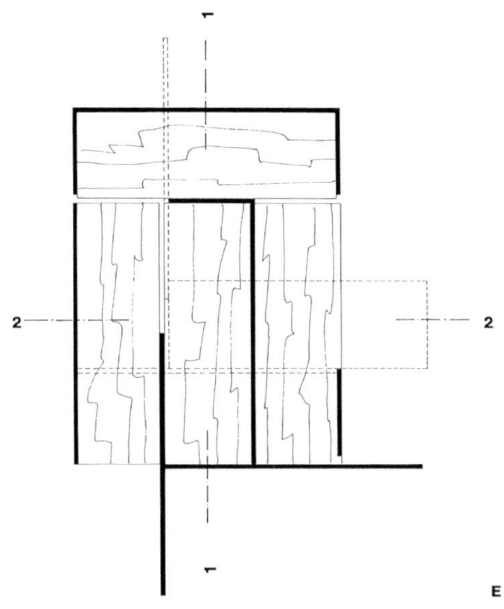

ERDGESCHOSS

ANSICHT 3

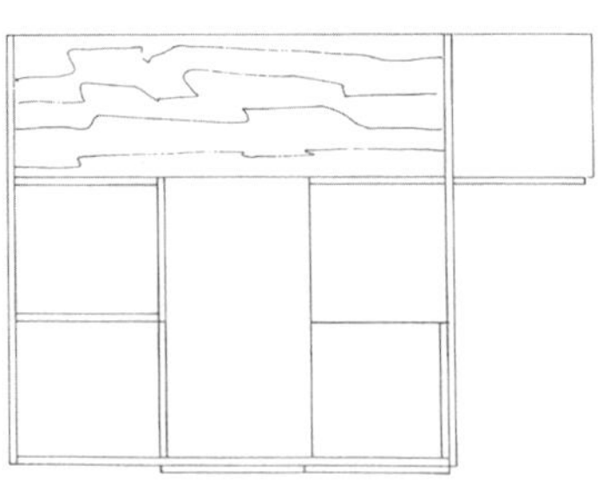

3s
Vienna
1993

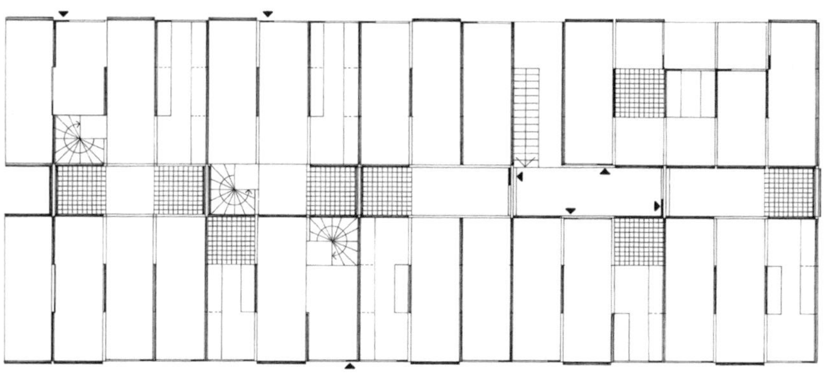

With a small number of large-format building components a rough, ready-made framework – like a house of cards – will be provided to the users for their appropriation and fitting-out. With *low-tech* means, pre-fabricated, rough 3s panels in the largest possible format and conducive to adaptation are quickly assembled in the shape of a house.

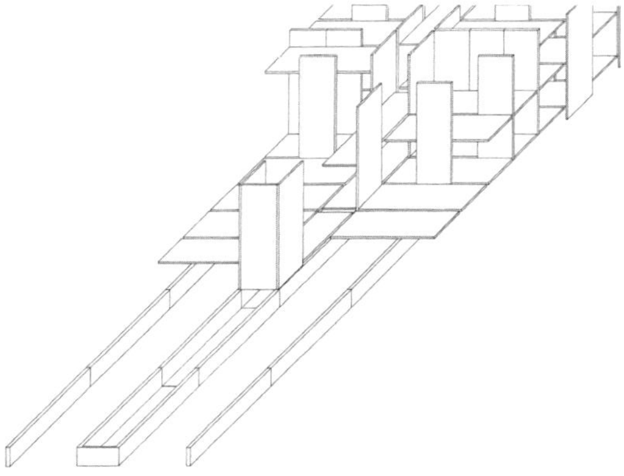

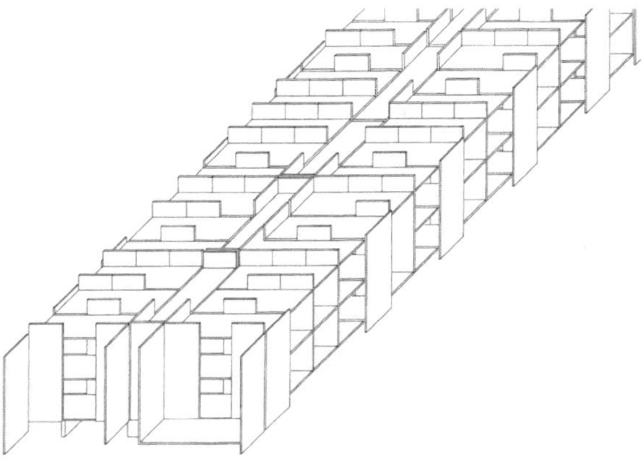

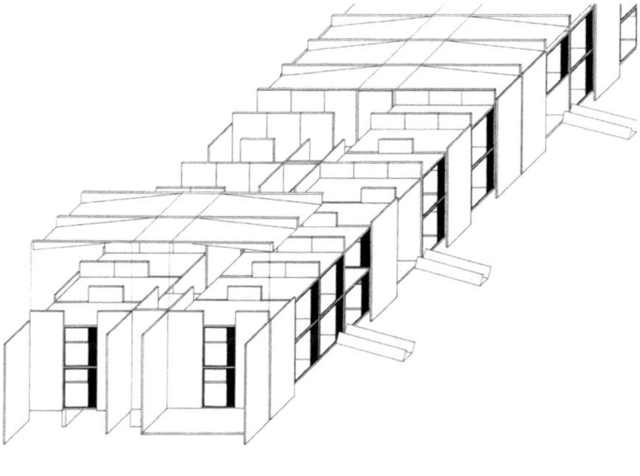

Lustenau Sand
Lustenau
1990

A concept for a basic 10×10 meter framework of solid concrete units was developed for a site in Lustenau; the framework is equipped with all of the required technical installations and is well-suited to being fitted out in lightweight construction. The small single-story dwellings arranged around a courtyard – each dwelling has a stair to a roof terrace above – can be enlarged to extend up to three stories. Make adaptations rather than move somewhere else.

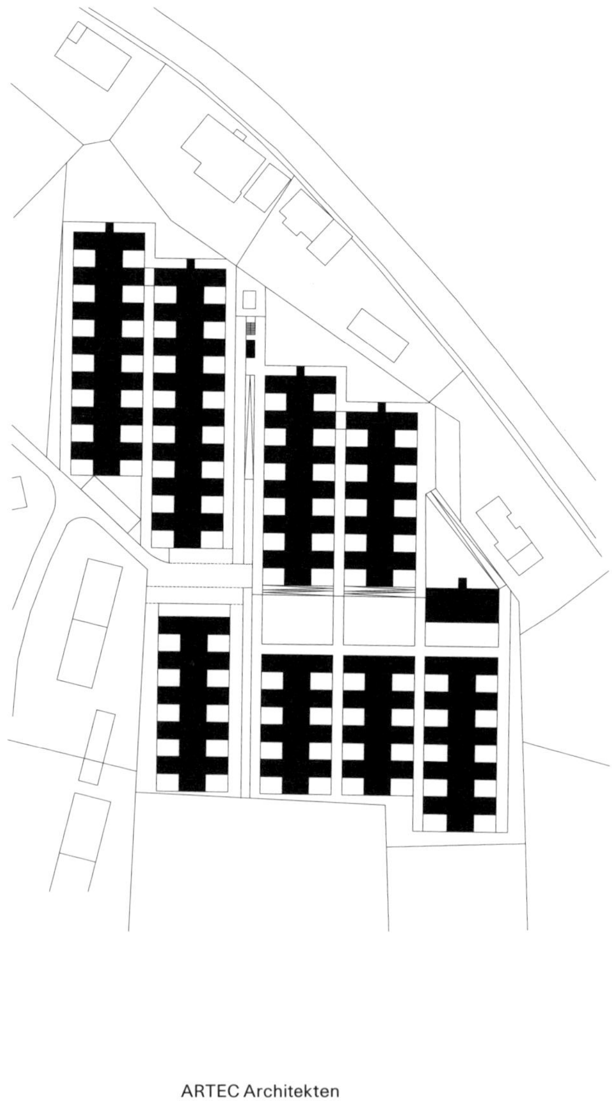

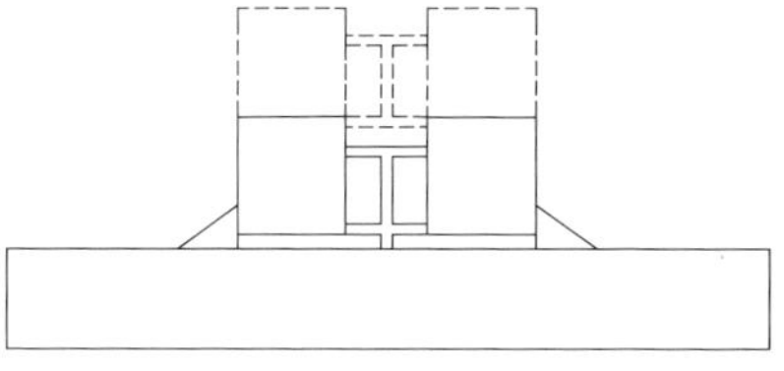

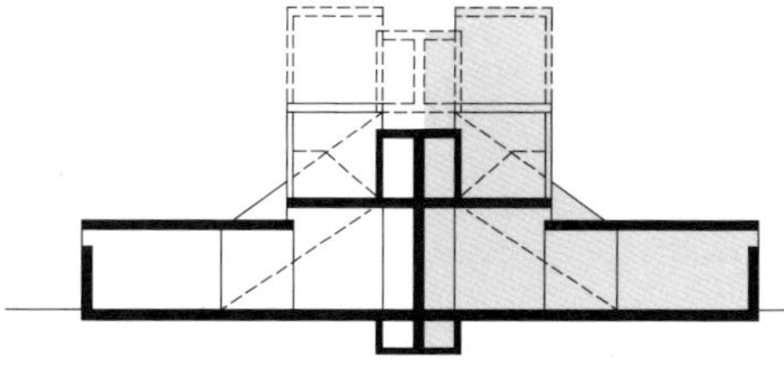

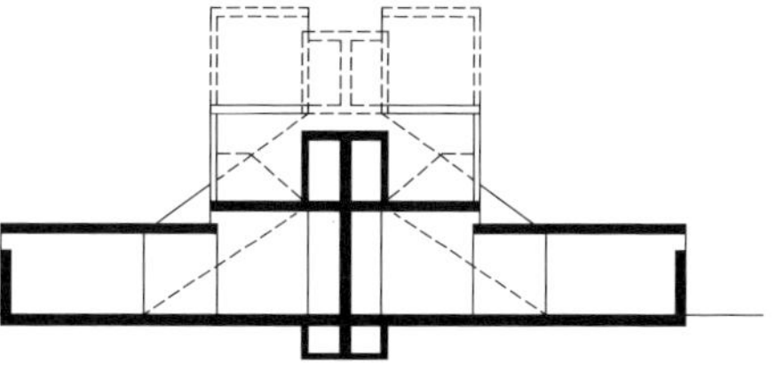

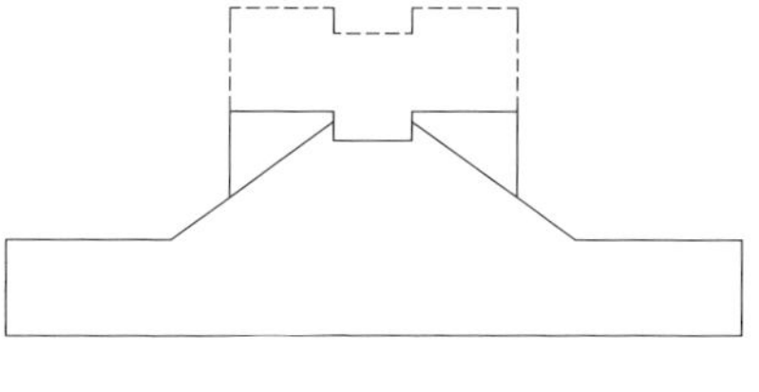

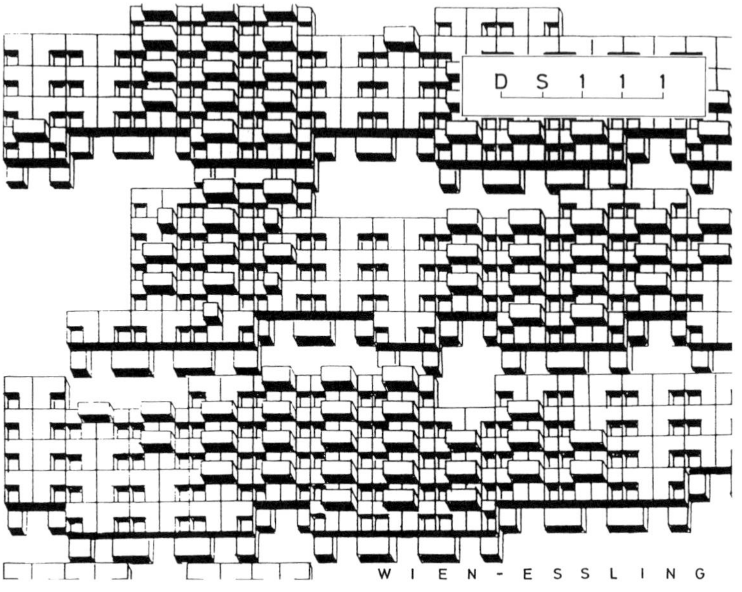

Essling – Europan 2
Vienna
1991

A concept for a framework for living with a 10 × 10 meter basic grid was developed for a site on Vienna's periphery. The housing units are densely arranged; as many as five units are grouped together in immediate proximity. From the streets running from east to west across the site, one drives underneath the raised ground level to one's unit and enters it directly from below – from the parking space.

What interests us about architecture is distinct space and the aspect of plasticity, architecture's almost inevitable proximity to sculpture. In other words, we engage with space in concentrated form, which, in the best case, calls forth – like a landscape can – a direct sensation that comes across as both matter-of-fact and surprising. Our intention is not to elevate nature, but to parallel it. What fascinates us about the spatial configuration of an object is its idiosyncrasy, not a neutral or indifferent character.

We call objects *sculptural* or *plastic* that exhibit coherence – whether they stem from the functionless realm of art, or from a technological discipline governed by laws. The sculptural impression often emerges in buildings that possess a pronounced structural component. Our work sounding out the potential of frameworks, the *typological* aspect of building, is one of our key approaches to planning: paring down and tweaking the tangible conditions to create possibilities for societally relevant solutions. We return to the principles or strategies that we have developed and in that way save our energy for what's essential. In the planning process, certain basic rules can be defined, so to speak, as preventive measures: using full-format materials, appreciating the right angle, using light to separate elements, materialization of the parameters, dispensing light as spatial experience, setting free the essence of the materials, pushing the surface to the edges, and giving precedence to the horizontal over the vertical.

Taking a typological approach as point of departure, our architecture becomes *distinct* through the concrete superimposition on a specific localized situation for which it was conceived. That is why difficult sites are of special interest to us: the more complex the parameters are, the more complex the solution has to be. But what is important is that the concept gives rise to what is built and that it not be *designed:* design is in that sense superfluous.

Spuller Residence
Vienna
1994

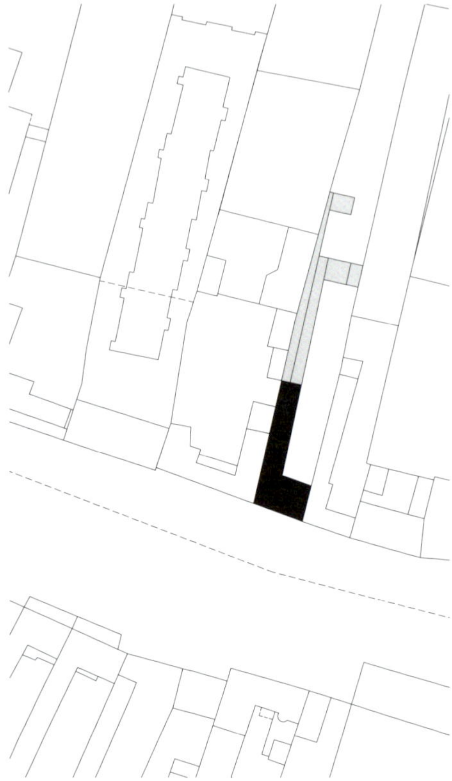

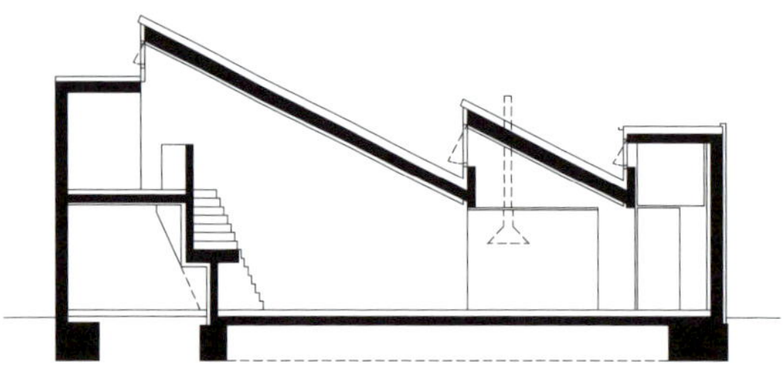

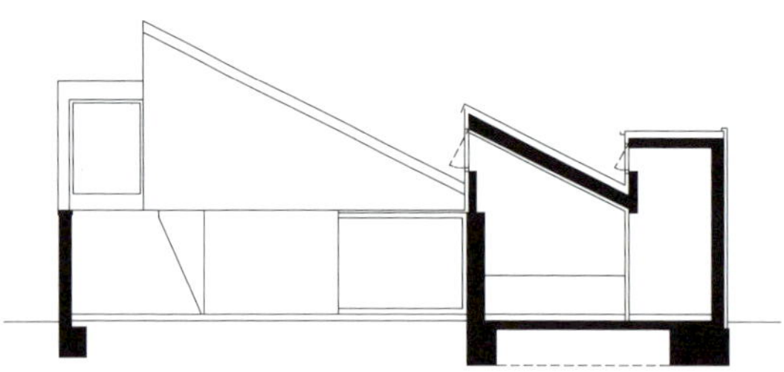

The introverted concept for a residence in what was once a “one-road town” was built on what is referred to in German as a “towel site” – a narrow piece of land which typically has L-shaped structures along the street – and the brief stipulated that it be enlargeable. The interior set-up of the house is based on layers (corridor, rooms, living area, library) lining the site longitudinally. Each spatial layer can be assigned the length it requires, whereby each room is provided with light from the clerestory windows in the shed roof, and therefore even the parts where the built fabric is most dense receive light from above.

Instead of the de/constructivist fascination with accidents, we seek out the complex beauty of the accidental. Concrete form comes about by way of an abstract thought process. There are many possibilities, but for each project there is only one best course to take.

Housing is our central theme. Not only because housing is the most frequently occurring typology, but also because it effects each and every one of us. To clarify which approaches play an important role in our line of action, we would like to outline three main thematic fields.

horizontal and vertical

At the beginning of our involvement with housing, there were two Austrian approaches in particular that interested us: Roland Rainer's housing complex in Puchenau (a suburb of Linz), an exemplary concept consisting of low-slung massing; it illustrates at a large scale how individual houses, in combination with garden walls, can be arranged such that there is a high quality of life, and, at the same time, bring about a compelling sequence of public spaces. The other project is the stepped-section building by Werkgruppe Graz in St. Peter (a district in Graz), a concept that functions similarly to a housing model devised by Herman Hertzberger: living units with adjoining outdoor spaces stacked atop one another, put together as a large volume in a highly plastic manner. The housing by Hertzberger and the stepped-section complex dating to the 1970s demonstrate how horizontal planes can be integrated in vertical layering. The circulation in the complex is open to one and all; "air stories" draw horizontal planes into the heart of the building. The apartments' adjoining outdoor spaces are varied in character, and the conceptual robustness and resilience in the face of private or natural inundation creates an experience that is more reminiscent of a landscape than of a building.

an urban framework
Vienna
1996

This concept for an unfinished building framework, which takes cues from the density and size (floor area) of the neighborhood's *Gründerzeit* buildings, was developed as an alternative to perimeter-block or linear building massing. The urban configuration is based on the main connections, which run from east to west at 110-meter intervals. The crosswise bar-shaped structures – width 10 meters, and 10 meters apart – creates permeability. Additional bar-shaped structures of the same size are superimposed perpendicular to these. Their height is 10 meters, whereby the distance between them measures 20 meters. Higher density is foreseen for the edges of the grille-like structure, where the economic potential is greater.

typological and topographical

For us, the essential *theoretical* approach to housing is typological. We seek to develop structures in a way that codifies in the buildings, so to speak, a certain spatial potential that we consider essential. This involves formulating serial, robust concepts that can withstand the superimposition of individual spatial requirements, specific local conditions, or influences defined by market-driven forces.

Our work with typologies helps us to find out what our affinities are and how a milieu can be produced that we find *pleasant, beautiful*, and livable. We don't think that it makes sense to try to deal with complex demands with a comprehensive theory. Thus, taking a typological approach as point of departure, we prefer a way of working in which the response to the context generates the design process.

introverted and extroverted

Good apartments can be conceived of both looking – almost exclusively – outward and radically introverted. It is more a matter of inclination, or of the approach taken, which is why we do not choose a stance early on in a project. What counts is simply that the relationship between inside and outside is as open as possible.

Construction of housing is, at present – perhaps it has always been the case – the segment of construction with the lowest standards and is implemented with the most meagre investment. On top of that, legislators have injected a profusion of norms and codes into the profession – regulating, for example, insulation and waterproofing – so that in subsidized housing it has become next to impossible to achieve a halfway acceptable relationship between the indoors and outdoors. Quality of life ranks far behind avoidance of condensation.

FA774

Europan 1
Graz
1989

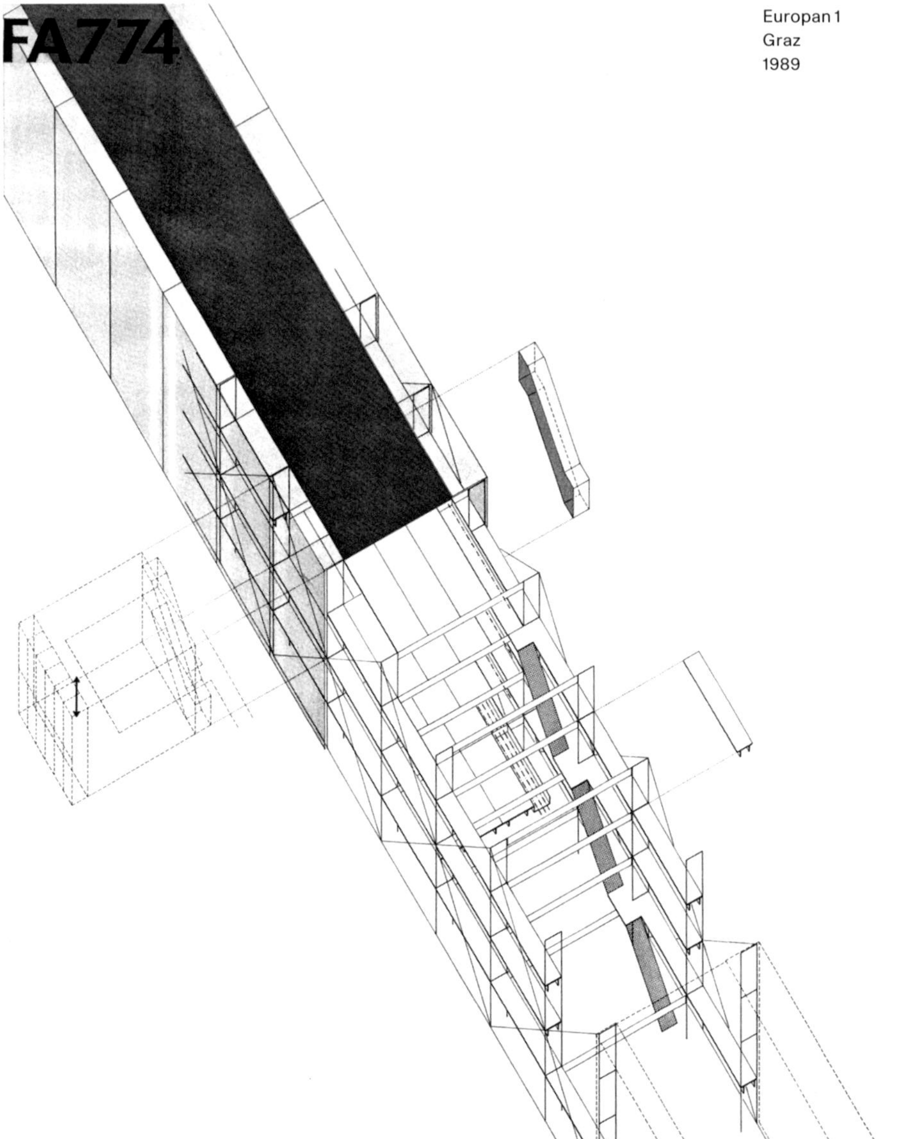

The typology picks up on the *Gründerzeit* treatment of urban fabric and superimposes upon it a simple, functionally neutral concept that is articulated as multi-story hall with no load-bearing intermediate walls, whereby each dwelling is oriented to the sun. The aim: to take a step forward, producing a building using contemporary means – a building like a refrigerator.

Since the baroque era the concept of *strong* space as a quality – as a fundamental notion – has enriched architecture. In the present situation, in which architecture is increasingly determined by economics, making provisions for spatial reserves in structures can become a subversive program for creating spatial characteristics and quality of life. Buildings with spatial reserves are in a position to adapt to – not yet known – future needs. This spatial concept and our stance, which asserts that a building should have more to offer to the general public than just its private functions, are further elaborated upon in response to the respective context. Building frameworks, developed as abstract concepts, constitute the grammar of our work – whereby the concrete context determines how they will be applied.

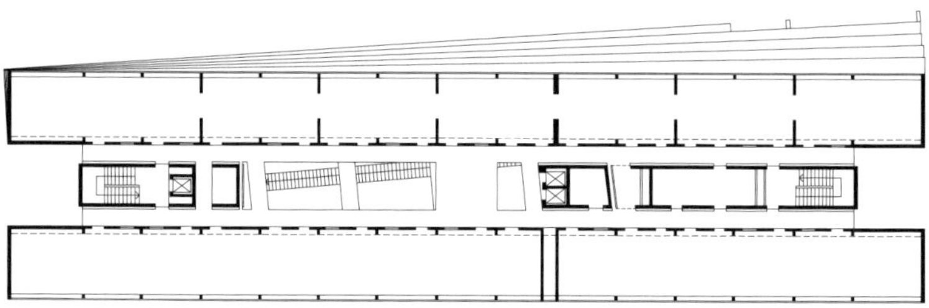

building authority
Graz
1988

Derived from the configuration of the site, the simple double-loaded basic conception has interior spaces that fan out. Stepping back on the west side, the top story again becomes parallel to the slab to the north. Widening the hall toward the west makes it possible to connect all levels with a straight set of stairs that begins at the main entrance. The cores – with elevators, stairs, and lavatories – are freestanding to allow light to enter the lower levels. On ground level, near the main entrance the building massing dissolves and become penetrable.

In: *UmBau 14*
Österreichische Gesellschaft
für Architektur,
Vienna 1993

The apparatus for form-finding, examplified by one segment of construction: housing

preview and two distinctions

Architecture is not something that can be solved once and for all. Nor does "form follow function," but rather function is a prerequisite – just as a roof should be watertight. We demand plastic architecture, in the sense of "less is more." Taking an abstract concept as point of departure, the less that can be eliminated without endangering the concept, the better the result.

first distinction

Our work takes two different approaches to dealing with programs: first, articulating form by way of content, from the inside out, or, in other words, the program turns itself inside out, and second, in contrast to the first, the *paste-up method* involving existing building elements (prefabricated units, existing spaces) or architectural working concepts in the broadest sense.

second distinction

Even in the late twentieth century, housing – with the exception of towers – occupies a field of tension consisting of *point – line – surface.* And, on the other hand, aside from its inherent appeal, the tower is not really in a position to be part of the solution to the housing question. Human beings move in a horizontal plane; vertical layering of horizontally organized levels does not allow a greater degree of freedom as heights increase. On the contrary. Circulation requirements, fire-safety measures, and structural specifications are major hindrances to an open spatial configuration.

the alpha of the housing question: the neutral envelope

Seen in terms of enabling a variety of uses and a workable building width, number of stories, and siting, as well as the employment of industrial manufacturing methods, what results is a linear massing type at the greatest remove to the plastic form-giving of the *use-blind basic structure*. It is based on the extruded-profile principle. The technical infrastructure is situated on the exterior along a longitudinal free space zone. Free in the sense of limitations of the structure, and open to later conversions – with the Centre Pompidou as prototype.

The different functions of the building enclosure should be kept separate spatially. By articulating and defining the outer skin – each element is

nursing school,
addition
Graz
1993

Every function is translated into a linear layer of the building, and each of these layers straddles a linking circulation space: classrooms, corridors, auxiliary spaces, etc. are inserted on a circulation path like tasty morsels on a shish kebab.

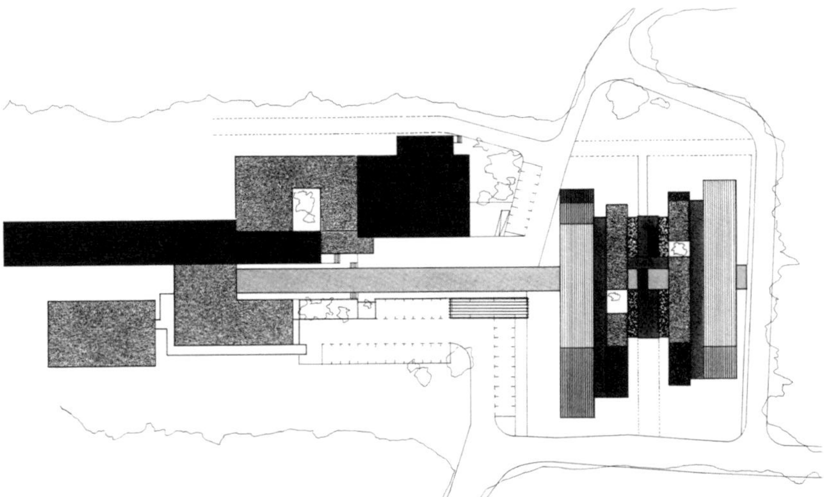

defined separately – we create a multi-layered interface comprising the functions *insulation/structural engineering/shelter*. This approach is radically on display at Mies van der Rohe's Farnsworth Pavilion: the house actually extends across the entire site. What is generally portrayed as an object in space is an icon that gives rise to misinterpretations and is in fact only one part of the barrier to the outside: protection at the outer limit, structural members on the box's exterior, insulation as definition of the envelope (= in this case, the box). In 1924, Hugo Häring stated that "A window has three functions: 1. to give light, 2. to allow ventilation, 3. to create a view out. ... What is to prevent us dividing the functions of a window and fulfilling them separately in the best way for each?"[1] One can apply this to all of a building's functions. The specific form-giving remains in the background as a diffuse possibility. We show the linear quality of the bar-shaped building, the beauty of the smooth surface and the play behind it.

the point as potential part of a series: the untapped texture

In the broad field of single-family-home construction, an additive approach is to be contraposed to the conventional solitaire building type. The individual building is viewed as a potential part of a linear or planar structure. The additivity requires a certain *fundamental introversion* – as opposed to reaching out into the landscape. Densification of contemporary single-family-home subdivisions is, de facto, nearly impossible. In contrast, introverted concepts which from the start include an option for direct annexation would definitely be open to it. Experimentation with prototypes – which goes beyond the self-realization of aesthetic concepts – is, so to speak, newly acquired territory in the quest to reduce land consumption.

the plastic quality of the bar-shaped building

In contrast to the content-neutral approach, here the program can become the form. By way of example, the bar-shaped building as abstract product, an embodiment of the current parameters for housing construction: the size of the dwelling is the factor determining the arrangement along the length of the massing. Our point of departure: we hold that the outdoor spaces – gardens and terraces – should be in proportion to the respective apartment size. The density typical of today's suburbs is attained with a basic framework made up of two-story structures; all residents can have a garden.

Prerequisite for broad bar-shaped buildings: all apartments are to be oriented to the south to the greatest degree possible. Topographic conditions or environmental parameters – noise, visual factors, etc. – can impede such an orientation. The basic framework has to be adapted

vocational school,
addition
Bregenz
1991

For an addition to a vocational school in Bregenz, the classrooms and workshops were organized linearly, stacked, and brought together under the roof. The workshops receive light f rom above via the special roof form – shed roofs extending farther downward than is typical – while the classrooms receive daylight through the facade. The *hedgehog-shaped* workshop roof gives the building its idiosyncratic identity and a scale that obscures the number of stories.

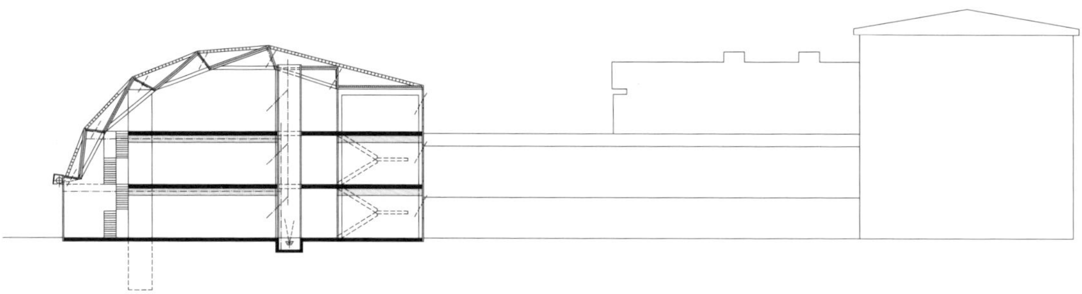

to the conditions like a custom-made suit: the meeting up of *general typology* and specific place gives rise to an individual configuration – as opposed to a simple product of set theory.

This is what is fascinating about historic cities: what remains is a spatial hull, a plastic sequence whose original *raison d'être* is no longer known.

bar-shaped structures, surfaces and surface areas

An exercise in surface area: a rough framework is superimposed upon the building site – this subdivides the site. The surface is to be appropriated to the greatest possible degree. According to Bernard Rudofsky, "North of the Alps, the courtyard house is considered alien. Instead, the front yard thrives – leftover from construction, no-man's-land, at best a meeting place for garden gnomes. ... A rehabilitated front yard undergoes a delightful transformation when a wall is put around it. Instead of shrinking, it develops optically and spatially; it rises up into the third dimension and furnishes a room with a celestial roof."[2]

If at all possible, semi-public spaces are to be avoided. Therefore, the enclosed spaces are structured intensively as efficiency apartments that can be extended or added to as needed. Residents can stay in place as their requirements change. Superimposed on the heavyweight construction (= hardware) is the anonymous fitting-out (= information). The property developer sets up a site with the basic equipment for living. External and internal qualities serve as a basis for living and dwelling – as an activity that is as heterogeneous as possible.

Putting an unfinished solid-masonry structure on offer is a rarity, but is nevertheless at regular intervals a peripheral topic, treated mainly as a multi-tiered building site, as a platform for do-it-yourself construction; in other words, a site for stacked homes as another option for multi-story housing (Eric Freiberger in Göteborg, Frei Otto's eco-house project in Berlin, a project by Yona Friedman in Marseille). Here the aspect of structure as primary element is brought to bear in a particularly striking manner – at once primary component and archaeological remnant, sediment of culture, washed ashore as historical jetsam.

yesterday – tomorrow. the amorphous figure

The house as incomprehensible construct, as three-dimensional event. The building as landscape, but *not* the landscape as pre-image of the building. The aim is to produce strong densification, and, at the same time, pronounced individuality. By clearly separating the functions *circulation* and *living* on different levels, the building moves away from being organized as bar-shaped massing and toward the plane, toward

Prado Museum,
addition
Madrid
1995

Point of departure for our project is the siting of the Prado on a topographical fault line within the city. As a building the Prado has a structure that accrued in layers over time; the structure developed to its present state out of the original core, which dates to the seventeenth century. Parallel to its structural change, the Prado's urban environment has developed independently of it. In this way it took on the significance of a solitaire in the urban context. Reconnecting the Prado to its surroundings and continuing to emphasize its special position are fundamental aspects of the concept. The urban approach seeks to redefine this space between the urban fabric and the convent as well as the lower-lying museum building by architecturally interpreting the edge of the terrain through the entrance building to reconcile the different levels and reformulating the urban space with respect to the building massing that rises in the west.

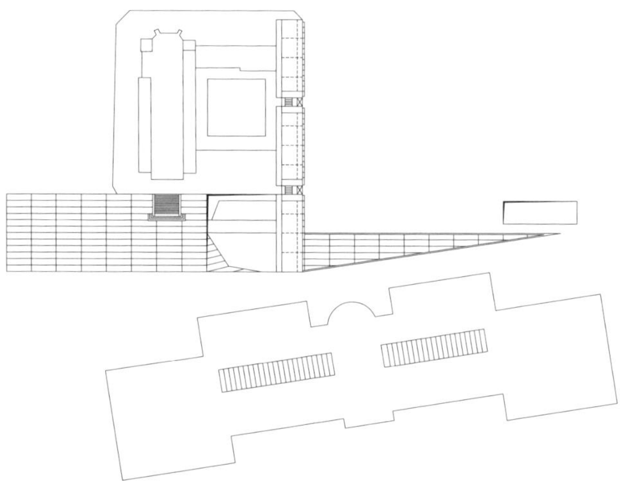

the *stack*. A technical grille above the access level holds all of the essential installations. The grille constitutes the basis for the *rampant outward growth* of the minimally equipped spaces. The notion of the space-city is to be brought to the level of the real. Unchecked rampant growth within a controlled system – in the sense of zoning guidelines of the technical sort. The structuring of Manhattan serves as an example, as does the Far Eastern three-dimensional definition of the exploitation of a buildable site.

conclusion

To be in line with heterogeneous requirements and contradictory demands, the building should be a machine. Open at the micro-level, the apartment floor plan, pronounced in its function as sheathing shell. It's not a matter of floor plan – facade – roof, but rather an understanding of the building as "firm skin."

1
Hugo Häring: Problems of Building, 1924
2
Bernard Rudofsky, "Der wohltemperierte Wohnhof," in: *UMRISS* 10, 1/86, 5.

II Openness, density, and the unfinished

The horizontal dimension is the basis for human locomotion. Therefore the classical categorization of a city's spatial elements is as banal and valid as ever: in the horizontal plane: the street, in the second dimension: the square; three-dimensional: the building. Urbanity – the city – comes about when these structural elements are connected.

The street is a linear, one-dimensional element that connects here with there. The street is a traffic route and bearer of infrastructure – indeed, infrastructures for the transport of water, gas, electricity, etc. are contained within it. But as long as no further element is added, the information level along the street's course remains minimal.

One form of a street's *informedness* becomes possible through the accretion of specific events – by way of buildings or squares. Over an beyond that, a collection of information comes into existence. The equipment generates possibilities for those who can *read* and use them – in other words, a *behavior*. The degree of informedness is heightened by the number of individual events intended for everyday use. Therefore, the cross-section of the transition from streetspace to the finite massing of the building becomes a main criterion for public significance – what is decisive for the potential of the street – aside from the number of buildings, and consequently, the possibilities should uses be changed within their life cycle. Examples include: ceiling heights and an openness to different uses on the ground level and the potential to enlarge the surface area by combining units. But an important moment in the accumulation of content occurs on the street itself, by way of seating options or different infrastructures. A different form of informedness comes about when two streets do not run parallel, but intersect: a second dimension is introduced, for there is a choice of goals. In the uniform accrual of these *intersections* a *grid* develops, an equivalent and sensible form of apportioning space, as consistent and identical basic requisites are created for connections of pathways or for the size of the parcels of land.

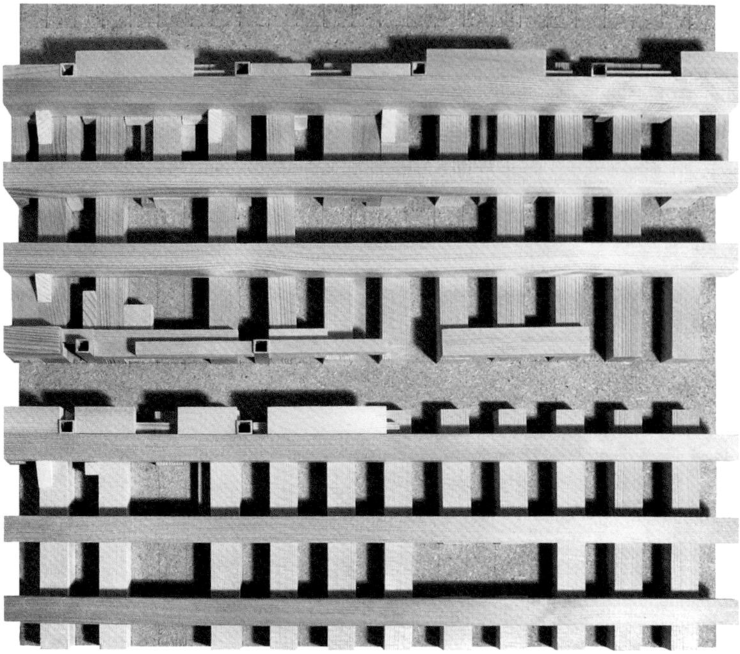

an urban framework
Vienna
1996

The *urban framework* is a concept for a building complex that takes its cues with respect to density and surface area from the *Gründerzeit* building blocks, but seeks an alternative to perimeter block development or to linear building massing. Special emphasis is placed on the potential of an unfinished space frame, which, on account of the 5-meter-high ceilings throughout the grille structure, is open to new uses, and the fabric, made up of housing, offices, and commercial structures, is conceived of such that it be accessible to the public.

In the *grid* – or fabric – the orthogonality of the urban threads is not the exception, but rather the rule. All other possibilities constitute anomalies, which came about despite the equivalency of the ground surface by way of the context of the buildings or the topography. The grid can be filled in in a variety of ways.

A third dimension in the usage of the urban grid is facilitated through the superimposition of built structures at several levels as well as by connecting them vertically. The advantages of short paths on the horizontal plane should therefore also be applied to the third dimension: a vertical densification, as is typical of buildings, can be applied to the city as a whole. This three-dimensional superimposition will become self-propagating and lead to the dissolution of outdated urban structures. Complexity in place of banality, thereby a quality of the streetscape, can come about by way of openness of the uses and flexibility of the structures in a dialogue between the building and the street. The street comes about through "solid" and "void" [Rowe and Koetter: Collage City], and the quality of a street is dependent on the degree of its informedness as it progresses horizontally.

When one speaks of *living*, particularly in a dense urban setting, one is also always speaking of inhabiting the city outside of one's own four walls. In other words, *urban living* means finding and defining strategies, typologies, and prerequisites for a highly densified, novel urban framework with a high quality of life. In our opinion, such strategies must be conceived of by way of a basic model that is as abstract and neutral as possible: for example, a grid framework that can be conceived of and elaborated upon not only two-dimensionally, but also spatially.

Successful urban models, whether European ones such as Barcelona, Paris, or Vienna; American ones such as New York; or Asian ones such as Tokyo, can be traced back to related structures. What differs is simply the spatial

Spark, feasibility study
Bratislava
2009

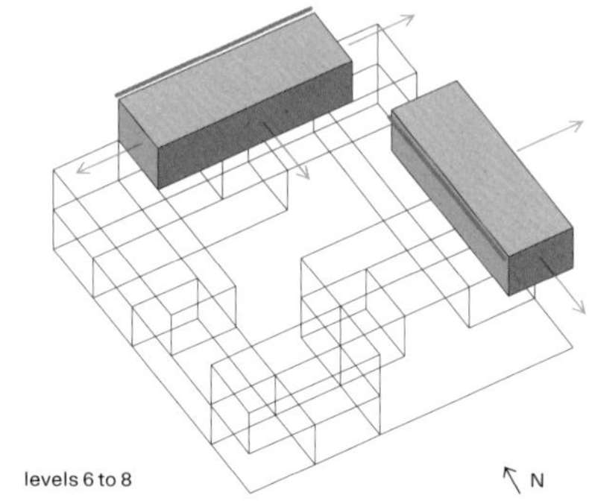

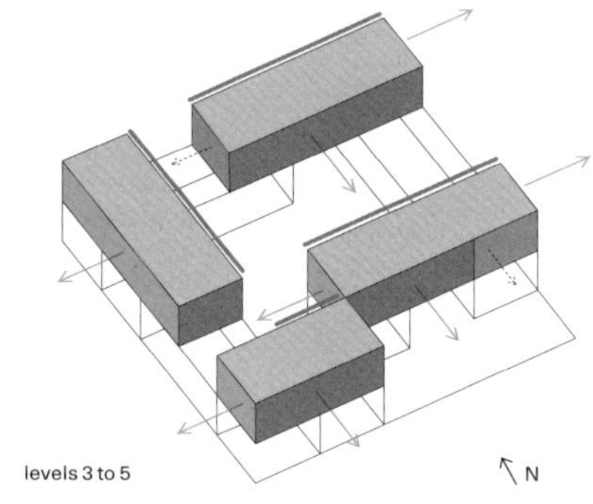

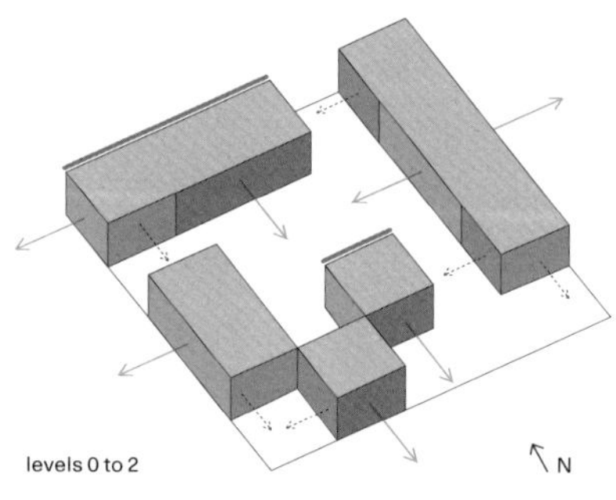

By introducing multi-story beam-shaped components, all with the same cross-section, and by steering clear of problematic corner situations, parcels of land can be put together as a multi-faceted urban structure.

This layering of components of different lengths gives rise to permeability and fosters identification with the district; it is not a matter of beginning with a complete figure and fragmenting it.

order as regards the height of the buildings. These more or less random – in some cases topographical – rules yield the highly specific characters of the respective cities.

In our view, analyzing, interpreting, and then once again abstracting these viable models is the fundamental point of departure in the quest for a new hybrid urban building block. The grid alone cannot be the solution; it is much more a matter of defining the places to be left empty within it, for what we are after is spatial and functional *air* – to allow for the necessary leeway in the building frameworks, the subsequent additions, insertions, conversions, intermediate uses, etc. – that individualizes the grid and makes it meaningful. Every growing metropolis should seek out development structures that possess *air* for future requirements: in other words, build frameworks that are, in the best sense of the word, unfinished, that enable free areas for a lively use of urban space. These uses are vital to achieving a high standard of urban living. If such offerings are lacking or are made impossible, the city has forfeited the advantage of having a rich offering of expanded living space. Then it's probably better to live in the countryside.

In der Wiesen housing complex
Vienna
2017

In keeping with our assessment that holds that density should be compensated for with added value, based on a preliminary study, a development concept was produced founded on the creation of porosity and of empty space. The ground-floor zone is designated a public space, while the upper levels are reserved for private use. To provide the minimized apartment floor plans with additional qualities, we conceived of the building such that a ribbon of loggias – with fronting balconies and extensive glazing – flanking all its sides creates a permeable atmosphere in the densely built-up fabric.

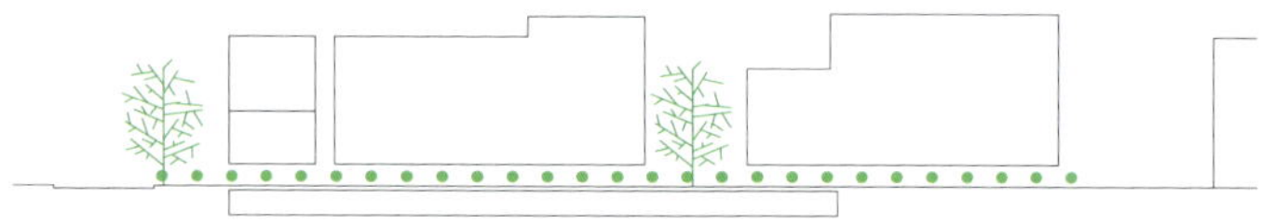

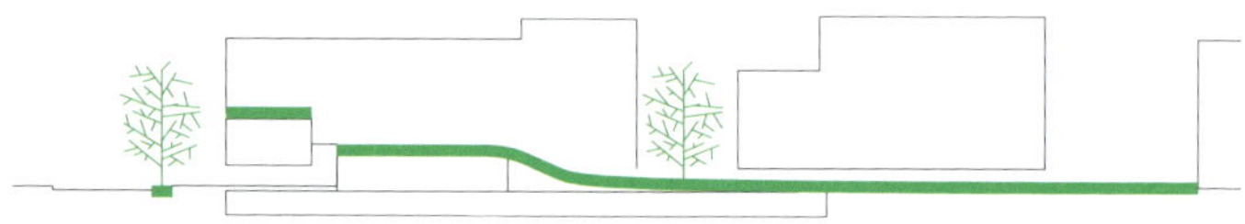

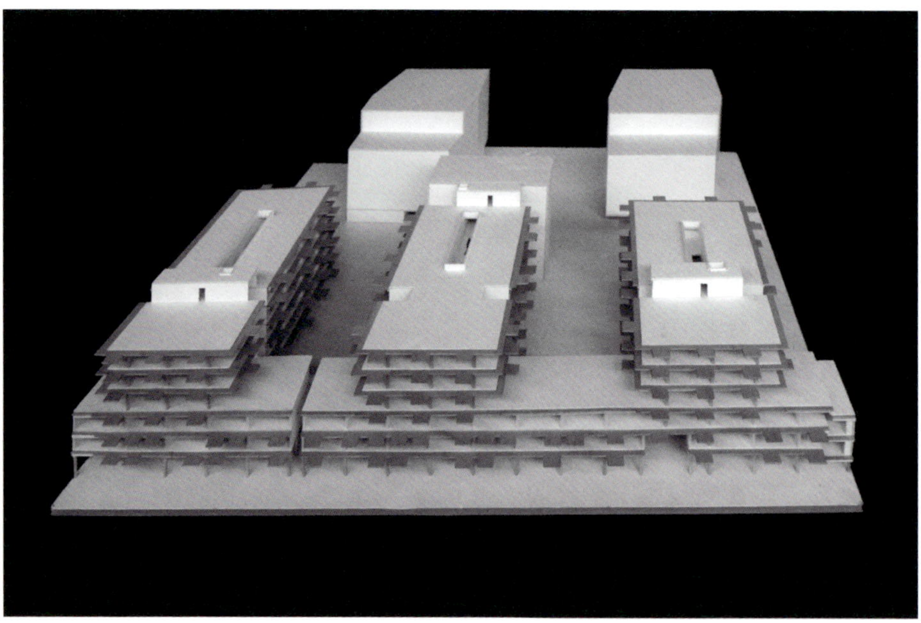

In: *Wohnen. Migration als Impuls für die kooperative Stadt*, Leibniz Univerität Hannover, Jovis, Berlin 2017

Living and ?

The need for housing has increased and the cause lies above all in the insufficient amount of building activity of recent years. In times in which there is a housing shortage and appreciable economic pressure on the size of the units and their standard, openness – as a quality – takes on new significance.

More and more, public space is being incorporated in daily life, and becoming in this way an extension of the living room. Therefore, we cannot limit ourselves to high-performance housing typologies, but must, above all, also address the accompanying architectural particularities of public space, in other words, with spatial qualities that evoke emotions and thereby make a city *specific* and memorable. To that end we need game rules that set up a balanced ratio between the amount of public space and the intended density and secure this stipulation as a fixed component of urbanity – the higher the density, the more public space. After all, a city is organized publicness.

The individual levels of use from public to private are to be linked by means of *thresholds*. These thresholds can be shifted, and can be re-negotiated and re-defined time and again. For especially at present – a time when the boundaries between living and working are becoming increasingly blurred – the question again arises as to how to link public and private realms.

The tendency is toward ever-smaller units, and the reasons for this are not only economic in nature. That would, by the way, be nonsensical, as small apartments are in reality more expensive than the larger ones, because the ratio of net floor area requiring shafts – kitchens and bathrooms – is higher. The only thing that can be reduced in the apartments is the *air*, in other words, that very part that makes an apartment *versatile in use* and relatively cost-efficient to build, comparable to the *Gründerzeit*-era apartments, which, though they are sometime a bit too large or too small, still always manage to function *somehow*. This *somehow* is charming on a number of levels, because it facilitates and allows for the unanticipated. This knowledge should be transformed into a new quality for an appropriable public space. The framework for a *public living* space is not a large or vast square, but, on the contrary, would have to consist of *niches, protrusions*, or *bay windows*, in other words, of structuring elements that, though they are known quantities, would require reinterpretation.

Conversely, the minimized apartment works well when the location of every element is pre-determined. Many of the conveniences or needs

apartment building
on Tokiostrasse
The Town Musicians of Bremen
Vienna
2009

In the dense package of different apartment types stacked atop one another along Tokiostrasse, certain spots were left open: facing the street, an arcade space was created at the sidewalk (bus stop) and as a continuation of the atrium that extends the height of the building. The arcade is kept free as a covered space for pedestrians and, longer term, as reserve floor area for future uses (shops, restaurants, club rooms, etc.). Situated parallel to Tokiostrasse, between the building lining the street and the courtyard-shaped building, is a space which, though its edges are defined, offers a publically accessible path through it.

On the ground level the project establishes a publicly accessible permeability; in the middle zone, an outdoor commons 7 meters wide and nearly 150 meters long; and on the roof, large terraces. In this way, despite the high density, the project provides added value spatially and potential for future developments. The airiness of the transverse connections contrasts starkly with the vertical circulation. The lattice-like framework makes possible a variety of paths across the site.

apartment building
on Laxenburgstrasse
Vienna
2001

of everyday life are unfeasible in these highly defined efficiency units, or carrying out different activities at the same time barely manageable. But cities grow, and sensible growth can only be achieved through densification. Because the densification of existing structure is only possible to a certain degree, the pressure to limit the size of apartments grows. *Efficiency units* only 30 to 40 square meters in size – but, as a consolation, in top locations – are a trend that can be observed in major cities around the globe. But that isn't surprising, because in desirable locations, typically in the heart of the city, public space that has simply grown and transformed time and again and been optimized over a long period of time functions well and thereby serves the function of an *expanded living room*. That's what we should orient ourselves to, because the higher the density and the smaller the unit, the more attractive, efficient, and versatile public spaces must be. By this we mean not only green spaces, but all public spaces, from the train station to the library. Our cities, and that includes all public buildings, must become more hybrid.

Though in most cities housing is clearly the *content*, housing alone does not produce urbanity. Once the ground floor is privatized, there's no going back, and that public space is lost forever. The *city* as large-scale system organizes the complex processes outside one's own four walls. In comparison, *living* is more simply structured, because our basic needs – cooking, eating, washing, sleeping – do not change at all, or only very little. But public space is the city's essential aspect, and it gives rise to special spatial characters that are determined by the day-to-day life and mentalities of the city's residents. In this way, emotional spaces that shape the *image* of our cities come into existence. It is these atmospheres that stay in our memories and define cities, for example, Paris and its boulevards or London and its front gardens.

Cities shrink or grow depending on the demographic development and the political context. As a structure that has grown over the course of centuries, the European city absorbs these processes and, despite the growth or atrophy, largely maintains its identity. It is this *elasticity of the urban figure* that distinguishes the city from buildings. A single building can be defined in its function by the client, but in terms of the urban structure, the building can never be *finished*. The urban structure must always possess enough leeway for the unanticipated, yet at the same time, create a publicness that fosters identity. There has to be room for this in new districts. This space is not functional and not quantifiable, which is why we call it *unfinished spatial reserves*.

pharmacy
"Zum Löwen von Aspern"
Vienna
2003

The pharmacy in Aspern's centuries-old core is organized as a house with a public path traversing the site from front to back. The space is conceived of as a transparent sequence that can be negotiated during opening hours and as a result becomes a constituent part of suburban life. In addition to this passage, a display garden was laid out on the roof, and seminar rooms accessible independent of the pharmacy were built. The latter are also used for public events. The superimposition of these different functions gives rise to the type of *social informedness* that we place value on when we develop projects.

The constricted site – wedged in between the elevated rapid transit line and suburban fabric – and the urbanistic context led us to develop a reinterpretation of exterior-corridor apartment buildings. The project's central element is a multi-story hall – with a vertical garden – which holds the vertical circulation. On the roof a terrace accessible to all residents makes up for the lack of green space on the ground level.

multi-generational housing
at Mühlgrund
Vienna
2011

A stance shared by three architecture firms determines the city-planning concept for the development of Raxstrasse, while the building massing is developed by each office independent of the others. This gives rise to a streetward appearance varied in character and to compelling outdoor spaces between the buildings. The permeability of the site to the public and the varied placement of the shared amenities play a role in creating a sense of identity and contribute to social cohesion with the surroundings. Our building was conceived of as a framework for neutral use. Non-load-bearing partition walls and a ceiling height of 2.60 meters on the upper levels facilitate future conversions. Two cores at the ends nearest the streets contain the main circulation; these are linked by halls (which receive daylight from above) and by broad corridor zones. The ground level´s ceiling height is 4.40 meters, an enhancement of the commercial zone. The roof is accessible to all residents and takes the form of a lushly planted sun deck.

apartment building on Raxstrasse
Vienna
2012

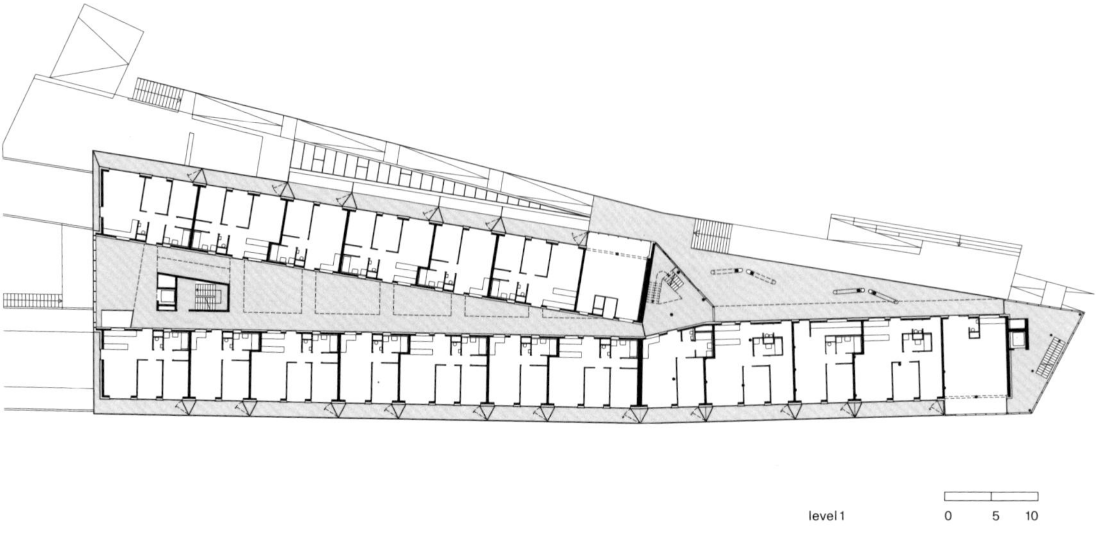
level 1
0
5
10

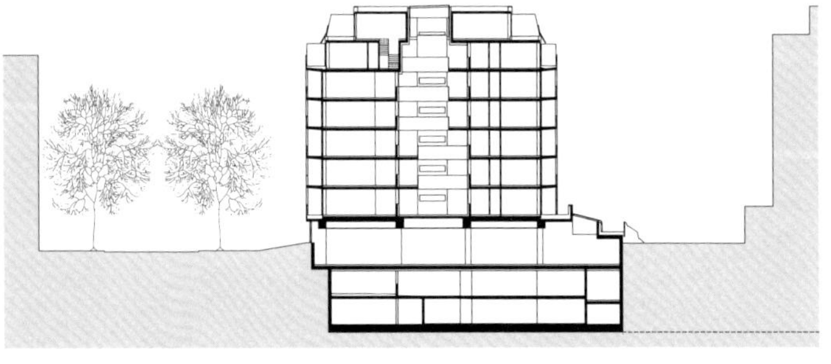

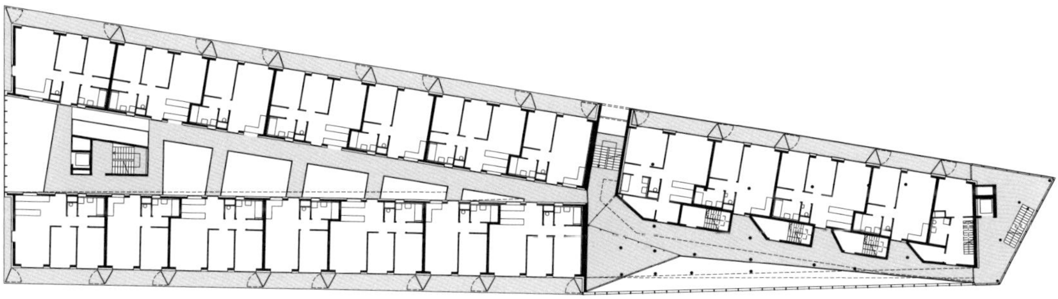

level 6 0 5 10

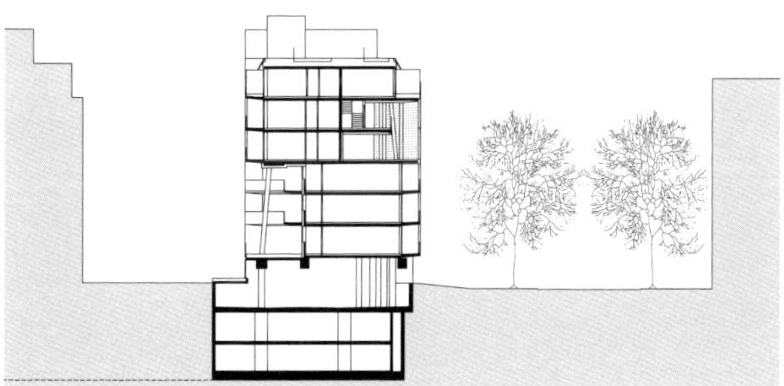

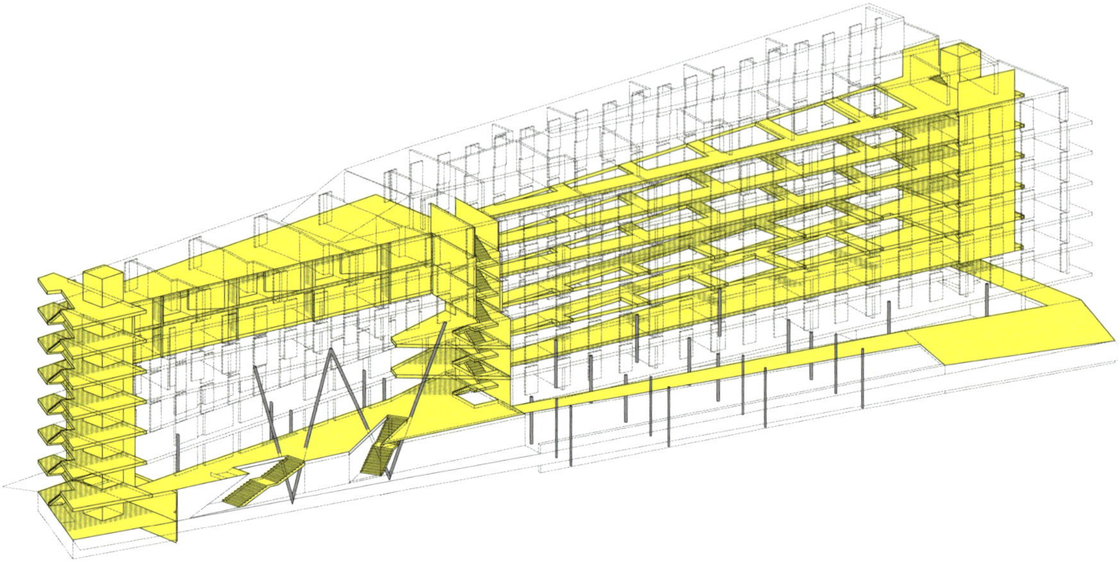

OG4
OG3
OG2
OG1

III

The plane and the framework: the contour of space

The floors, walls, and ceilings are fashioned of panels – with a proportion of 3:1 and all the same size, taking a basic ordering principle as point of departure; three longitudinal panels, one crosswise – making possible a free spatial arrangement of the elements.

Fuzzy House
Cologne
1993

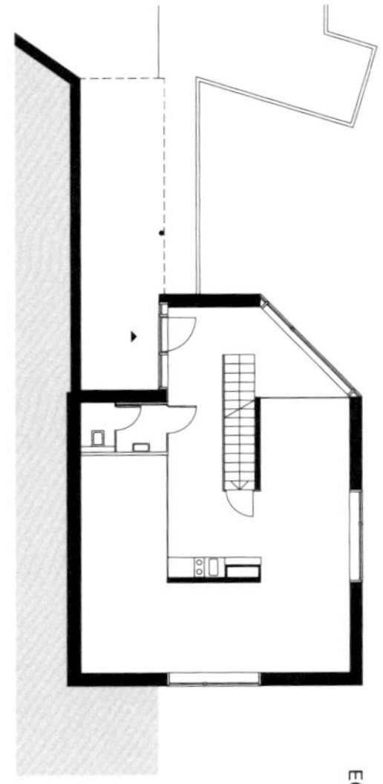

EG

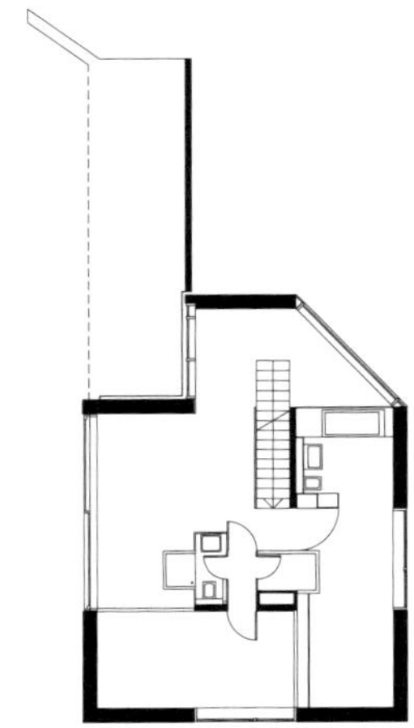

OG 1

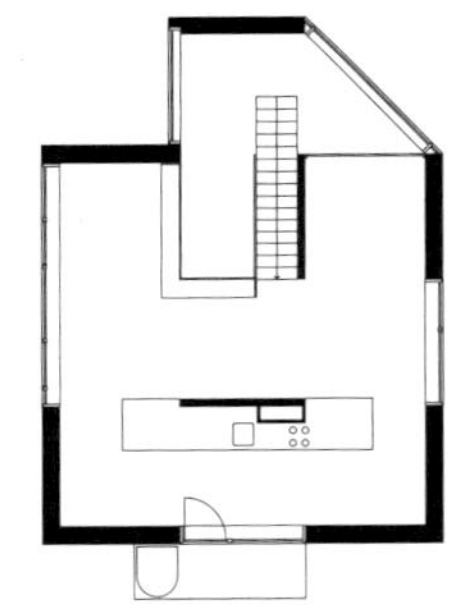

OG 2

A system employing three panels with a proportion of 3:1 was selected as a basic ordering principle. From it we developed a two-story cube, with each edge measuring 840 cm, in which the load-bearing structure is executed, both in terms of geometry and production, as standardized, partially prefabricated house. A simple rule yielded a spatially complex structure: in the floor plan the middle panel is shifted outwards – the 280 cm shift is equal to the width of the panel, but the joint that is created is enclosed with the exterior wall. All openings and the apertureless exterior walls are derived from a 280 cm grid. Core-insulated, precast concrete units and CLT panels serve as structural elements. The exterior walls have two wythes: the load-bearing inner wythe and the thinner outer one – the latter untreated. The floors, of precast concrete units, are – where there is no additional floor assembly – sanded and waterproofed. Large-format post-and-rail elements made of larch – and clad on the exterior in black aluminum – frame the glass facades.

systemhaus 2
Hörbranz
2009

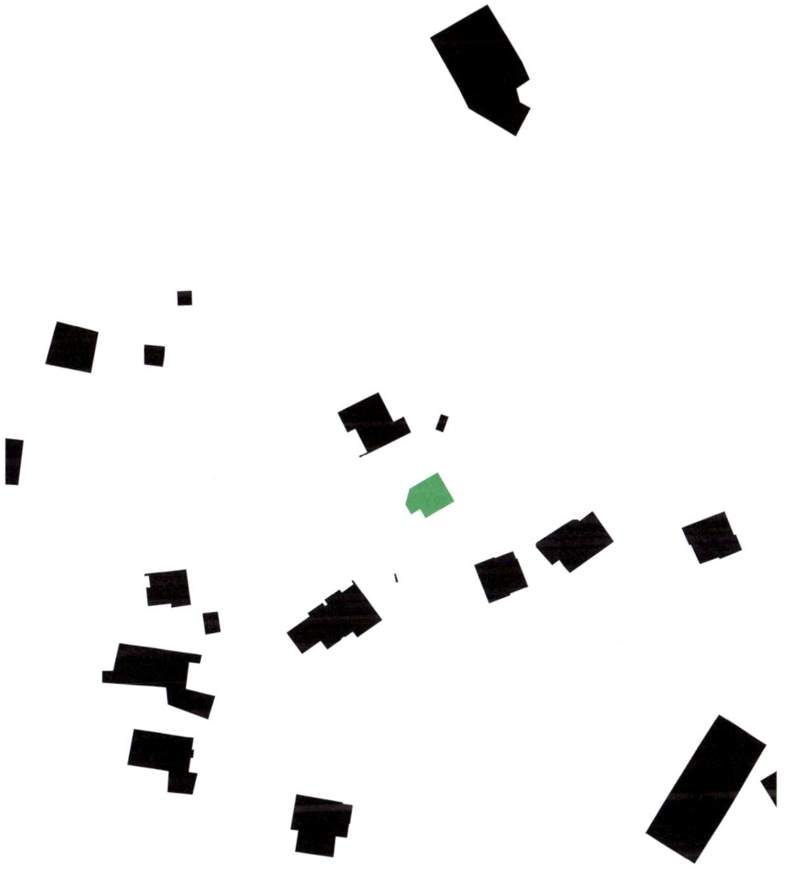

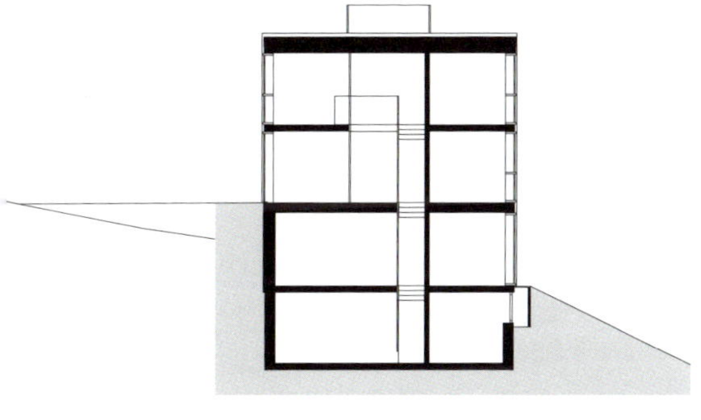

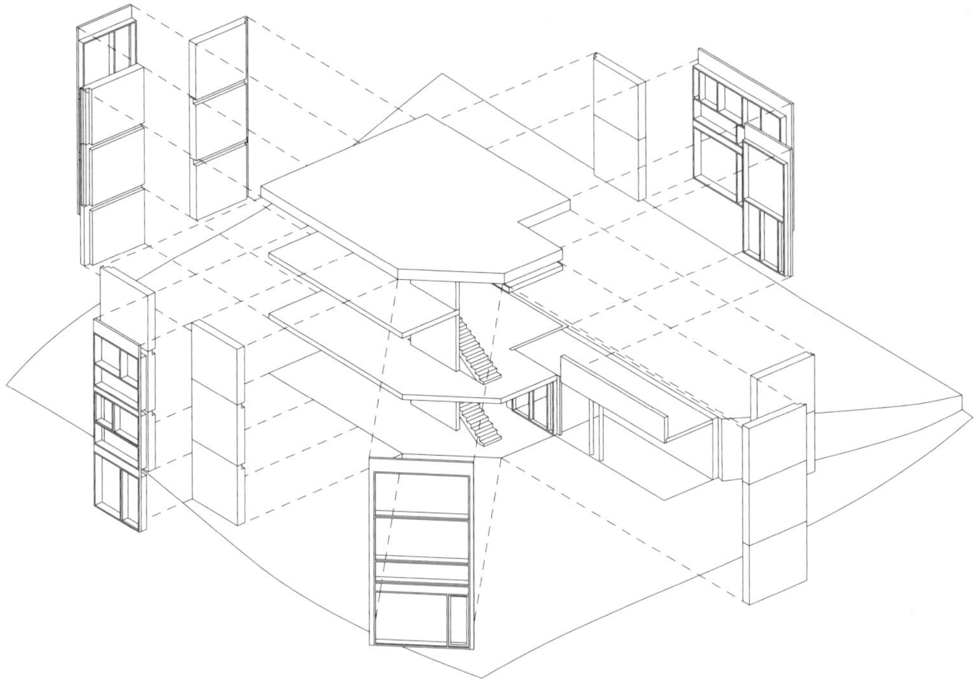

The property to be utilized for the holiday home extends from a little-used road via the crest of a hill with a view southwest to the sloping hillside. The house consists of a large space (60 square meters) for the owners and a guest room half that size. The units are linked by an open space between them that, with the assistance of sliding doors, can be transformed into a communication-fostering buffer zone. The two boxes rest on a deck; above them is a roof equal in size to the deck. The roof's overhang shields the house from direct solar radiation and thus keeps it from overheating.

B-B Residence
Bocksdorf
2005

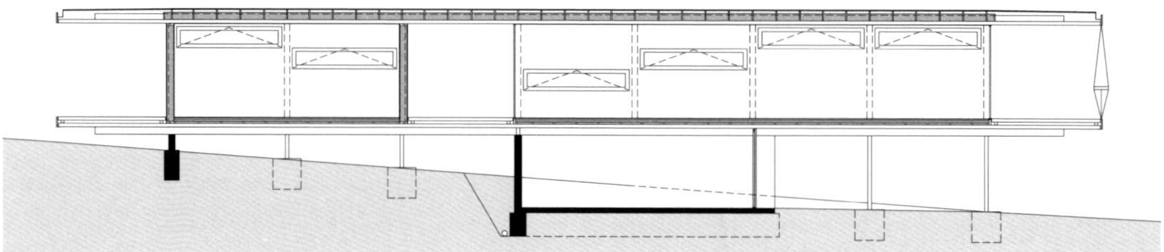

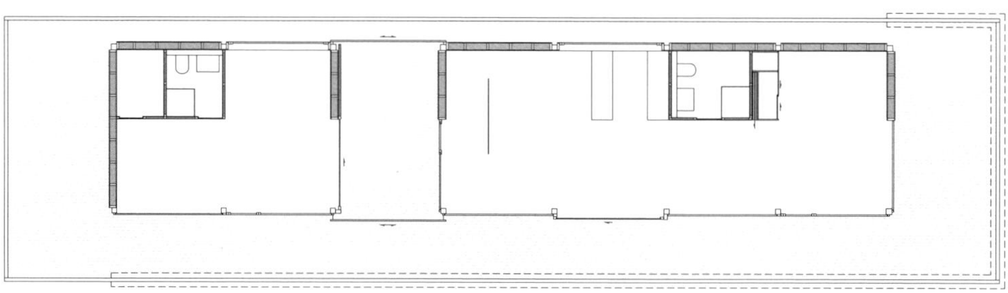

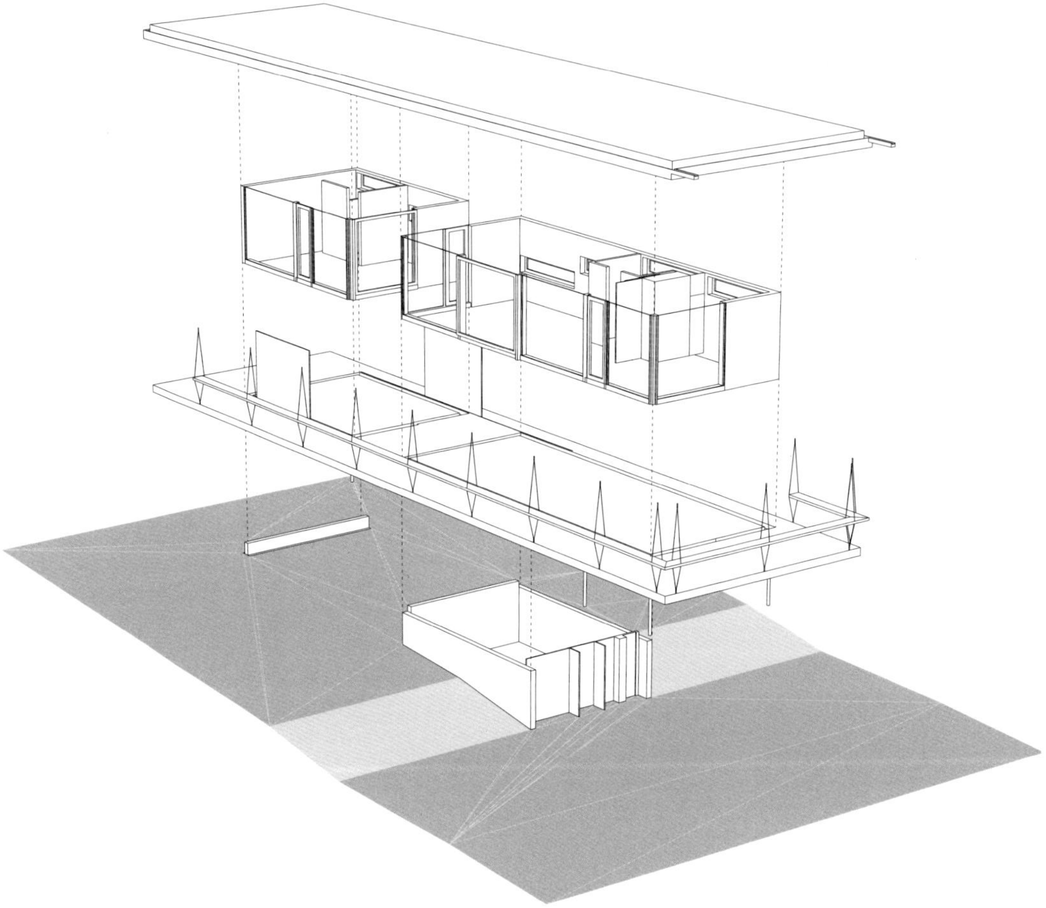

A farmhouse, consisting of a main building in heavy-weight construction and a shed in wood construction, stands on a gently sloped hillside. A new, largely pre-fabricated wood structure replaces the shed. The building is positioned crosswise to the slope and bisects the long site at its narrowest spot; covered terraces front the building on all four sides.

The wood construction of this new building corresponds to that of the nearby B-B Residence. The removal of the roof from the existing main building creates a further large terrace with vistas of the surrounding landscape – a supplement to the existing and newly introduced low-slung massing.

S Residence
Bocksdorf
2005

Architecture requires thinking in three dimensions, and this must be combined with craftsmanship. The craft of architecture is revealed in the detail. The detail may be described as the transition from one planar condition to another. In the fine arts, painting, for example, deals with the plane, the drawing of a detail, or, to be more precise, with the fault line between planes. The articulation of a detail defines the structure of a surface's form: the term *detail*, as something transcendent, as a phenomenon of the transition from one state to another in contrast to the uniform progression of an *assembly*, a situation in which requirements change. A specific way of articulating the detail is the prerequisite to differentiation of the design and the building in a homogenized world. The arbitrary applicability of a wide range of ideas of form which are presently ubiquitous thanks to the possibilities of data processing, makes one think of a new classicism – any thing can be used by any one any time. Aside from the spatial application – or perhaps, spatial invention – the detail, in combination with the load-bearing structure, remains the means to achieving authentic architecture.

We often enlist structural provisions, such as the use of grid systems, of standardized planar building components, or the decision to pursue simple stacking concepts as point of departure for a design. Instead of the 2:1 proportion of the tatami mats used to determine the floor plan of the traditional Japanese home, in our concepts we use 3:1 to establish the dimension of the floor panels and upright panels. And our approach to housing concepts – which usually are based on a 10 × 10 meter grid, and from which the dimensions for the individual apartment floor plans and the accompanying private outdoor space as well as the apartment units can be sensibly and functionally optimized – takes a similar path.

In our view, there is a fundamental distinction between *monolithic* construction methods and *tectonic* construction methods. Generally speaking, the difference

A *hall for living* with ceiling heights of 2.80 meters is inserted in a prefabricated primary structure of horizontal floor decks – reinforced concrete columns, and a filigree ceiling system. The circulation system is conceived of as part of a vertical urban landscape that leaves ample room in front of the compact apartments' doors, and thanks to the balcony zones, creates space in front of the facades, as well. The fire-resistant concrete floor decks make possible a ventilated facade in wood-rail construction. In this way, the floor plans that were optimized economically, yet are still versatile spatially and functionally.

apartment building
on Maximilianstrasse
St. Pölten
2017

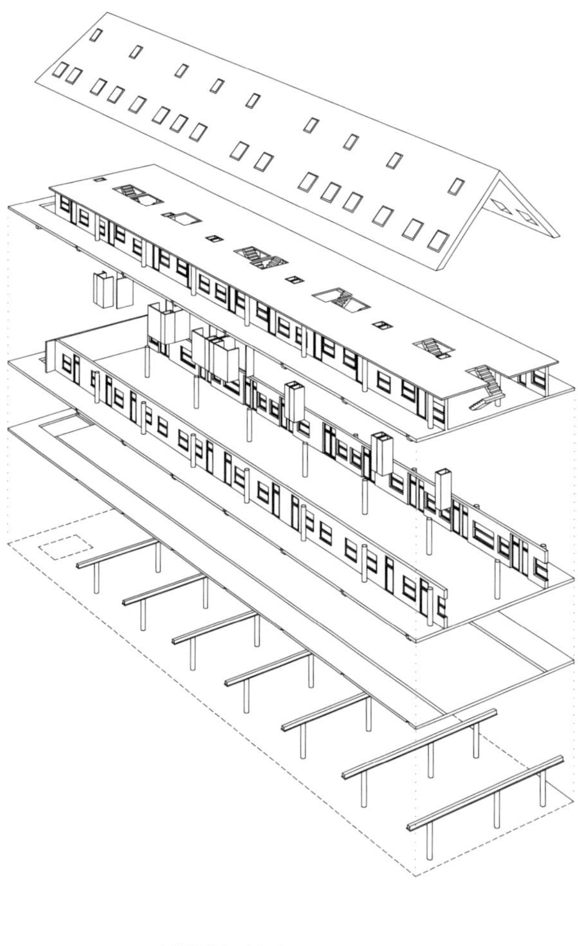

lies in the fact that monolithic construction relies on a single type of construction – in other words, requires no supporting structure.

The image of the fire-damaged St. Stephen's Cathedral, reduced to its space-defining material, clearly illustrates the intention of monolithic construction: the building has relinquished nothing of its impact, but instead becomes *sharper* still – without losing its singularity and quality. Although the building was erected of small components, its massing appears to be of one piece. The baroque era was no longer interested in this notion; its theme is space.

By way of simplification, one can say that structure is architecture's anatomy, whereby for us structure refers not only to structural engineering in other words – the skeleton – but also to the building's entire inner workings. If the organization of the individual building blocks – in other words, material (bones) and buildings services (nerves) – can be brought in tune with the intended use, a *soul* comes into existence. And when we say soul, we mean architecture.

In light of these aspects, in succinct terms, the following proposes a broad classification of materials employed: construction in concrete, which basically conveys a certain heft and finality; construction in steel, the expression of intellectual planning; or construction in wood, which, as a *simple* and ready-to-use product can be employed extremely versatilely. Taking the material as point of departure for the design process of a building essentially pre-ordains the detail decisions. Because for us the overarching concept of a building determines the material to be employed, the material determines the detailing, or, in other words, is a constituent part of the overall concept. Hence, decisions for a project occur as a consequence of the concept and are not individually designed: this brings about a spatial creation by structuring buildings with their programs and leads to pared-down aesthetics, because separate solutions to similar problems

The apartment is located in a former governmental administration building in Vienna. The building's structure is generously scaled, as are the ceiling heights. From the apartment entrance to the exterior wall, a cabinet made of oak separates the private and public realms and fulfils a variety of storage functions. The perforated room divider can be closed up entirely, or can be used permeably. At the entrance, across from the wall of cabinets, is a leather bench which extends around the corner to the kitchen. The kitchen's spatial definition allows for different settings – from open to closed.

apartment P.
Vienna
2016

are a waste of energy and resources. As simple as possible and as complex as necessary. The ambiguous effect of building components in one and the same context, as opposed to clarity.

An interesting topic is the moment in which structure creates *space*, an aspect of structure in which more is going on than the pure distribution of loads, with the obsolescence of homogeneous-monolithic construction – which required only one material – in *modern* architecture, the envelope is an applique. There is no such thing as bad material, but a lot of material is used incorrectly.

Kunstraum art space
Fischer Wing
Museumsquartier
Vienna
1994

The aim of the design for the *Kunstraum* was to develop a spatial framework that could be used flexibly for working and exhibiting, as well as for lectures and discussions. All space-defining elements are designed to be *devise-like*. That means that the walls can be parked or enlisted to create space.

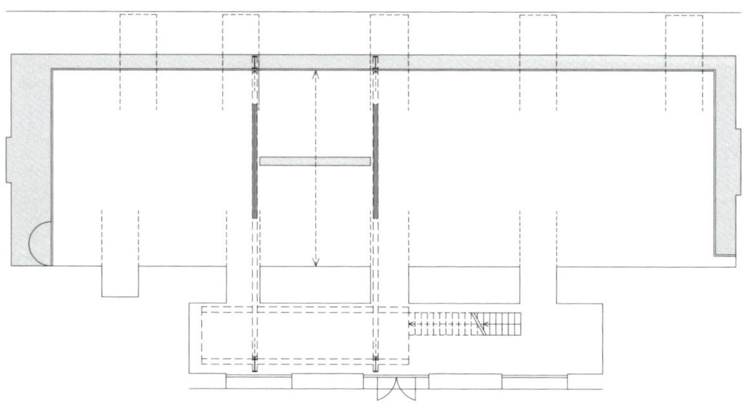

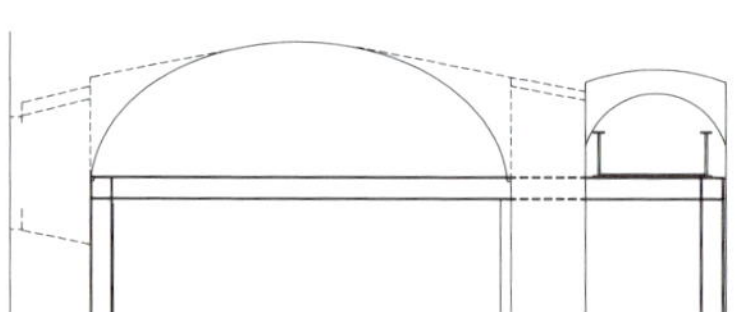

Depot, Fischer Wing
Museumsquartier
Vienna
1997

Following the closure of the *Kunstraum*, the Depot was built using the same elements that had been employed for the Kunstraum. The Depot is primarily a venue for cultural programs; this fact made it necessary to *re-structure* the individual building components. All of the Kunstraum's furniture was also reused – in some instances in adapted form and arranged for new functions.

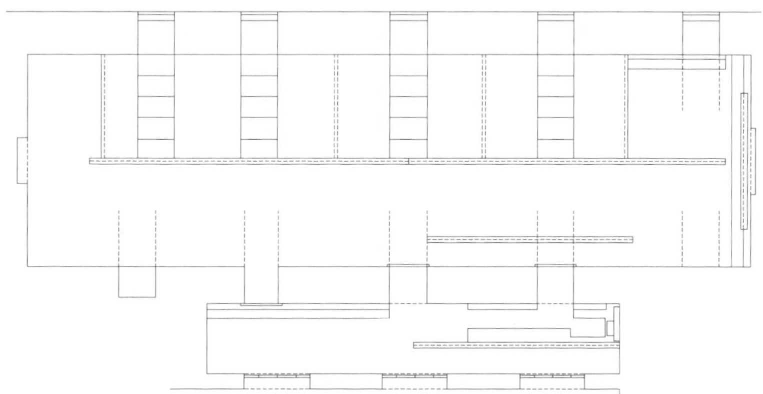

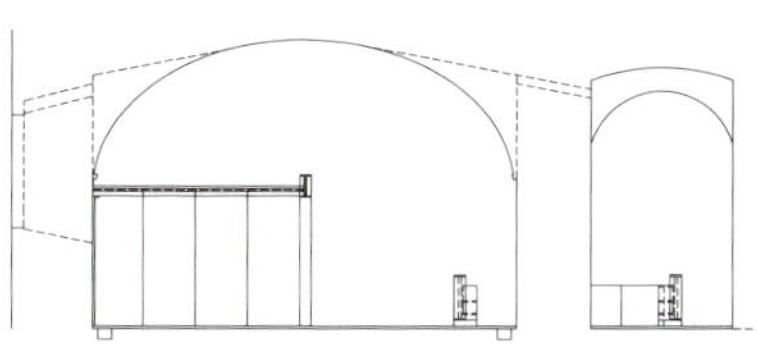

Maria Lassnig Foundation
Vienna
2017

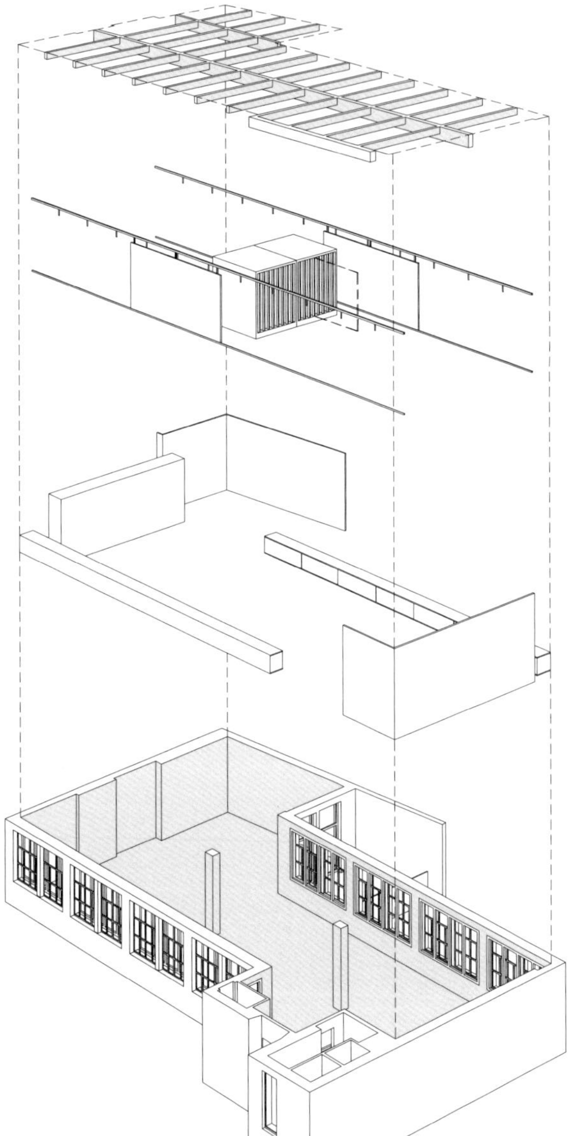

The spaces artist Maria Lassnig once used as an atelier are to be converted: the Maria Lassnig Foundation will use them as a depot, and as processing and exhibition spaces. The entire extent of the L-shaped studio building, an early example of a reinforced-concrete structure, is being shaped into a readily adaptable enfilade of exhibition and event spaces that will, at the same time, serve as storage space for the paintings.

The combination of exhibition walls, repositionable along the two windowed walls containing built-in stowable furniture, and storage boxes for the paintings – which can be arranged freely in the space – makes possible a variety of spatial configurations.

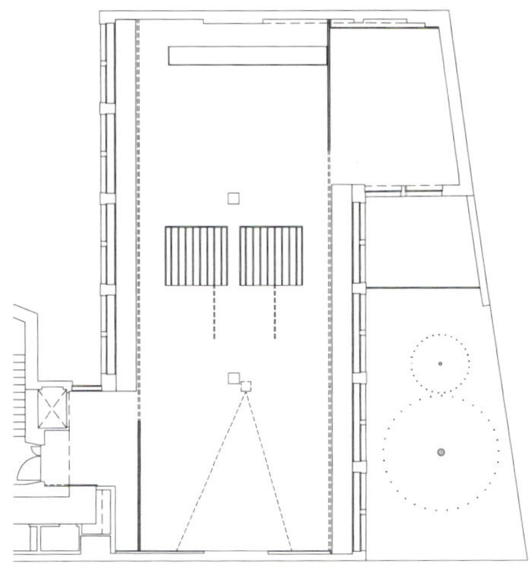

swimming pools in Schruns-Tschagguns
Tschagguns
2006

The concept, based on a 10 × 10 meter panel grid, creates an artificial landscape which, on the one hand, constitutes the indoor pools' spatial definition, and, on the other, provides a *lawn for sunbathers* as well as other leisure spaces for the outdoor pool. The modulation of the roof surface allows daylight to enter the space in different ways and creates a variety of spatial qualities for the therapeutic pool and the family pool.
The different outdoor spaces also have different characteristics.

Having reasons

Lecture held at the Festwochen Gmunden, 2016

"Having reasons," says Franz Schuh, "is the pride of philosophy." Architecture, in contrast, has ever fewer reasons – both literally and figuratively. In the literal sense that means, considering that potential building sites will soon be short in supply, that enough has already been built and that in future it will, by and large, suffice to make adaptations to the existing building stock. And architecture lacks good reasons, the motivations, the justifications, why a building is as it is. But architecture needs content. One could now say that that's obvious, of course in the case of architecture, the *content* is always also the brief, in other words, it specifies surface areas and functions, which, as a consequence, allows for the quantification of size, and, in turn, the costs of the building as expressed in cubic meters. Otherwise a building would only be an expression of the functional diagram and our built environment would be extremely dull.

Josef Lackner's explanation of why a building has significance over and beyond its function: "Ideas should determine our deeds. Architecture expresses ideas – and even though these are often lacking, one builds anyway. In this case, the idea not to build would be the best one."[1]

We architects, in other words, also need a *theory*, a basic concept, or put differently, content in the sense of a program, of a vision, of renewal of existing rules. Only when such a background exists can something come into being that we treasure and love – namely the emotionalizing quality of space. That is why we travel to foreign lands and cities and have a penchant for visiting what has been built there – be it churches, museums, apartment buildings, squares, or what have you. But the uniqueness and noteworthiness of spatial manifestations always also has to do with desires and demands – in other words, with content – but also, of course, with the mentalities of the architects and the users.

Because built architecture is always tied to a public or private need, working with architecture's content is essential. Particularly when the commissions are public, the guest to define the content over and beyond the simple schedule of functions, though demanding, is crucial. Exceptional architecture only comes about when the architect and the client can communicate on equal footing. But to accomplish that, the client also must have knowledge of the field – in particular, when he or she represents the public sphere. Not only in a whodunit does the storyline play a decisive role, but also in the case of architecture, a radical program is already *half the battle*. And policymakers must (also) take part. Because, according to Hermann Czech, "Architecture cannot

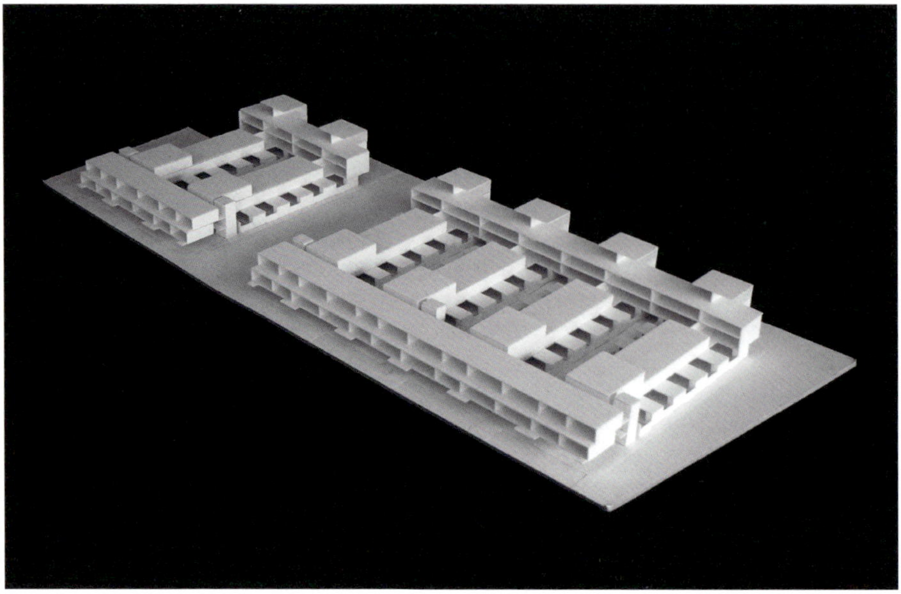

housing on Fritz-Kandl-Gasse
Vienna
2017

On account of the specifics of the site on the edge of the built-up zone – at the transition to green fields – we proposed a concept with extensive vegetation throughout the site and different levels of density. Its aim: to be a place that is welcoming to families and children and a place where through the inclusion of gardens and terraces the relationship between inside and outside assumes an important role. This allows residents to enjoy both lush surroundings and the conveniences of a city expansion district. Parking is on the ground, below the units' living-room level.

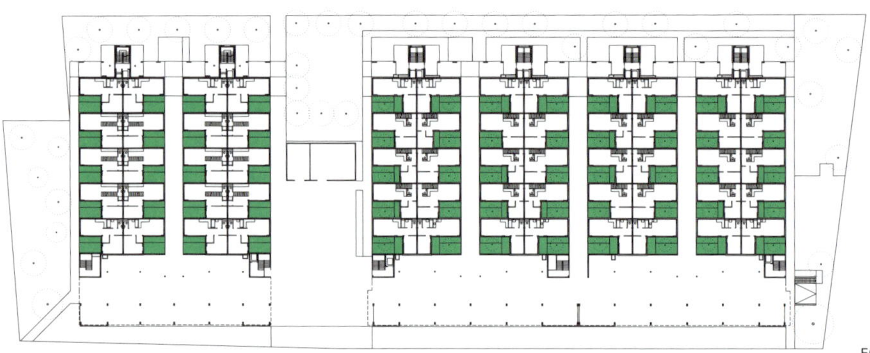

EG

place itself outside the system; realizations require it to have a powerful segment of society on its side."[2]

Building sites *come into being* today in a realm situated between politics and regional planning. But city planning is lost to us architects. Regional planners without a – content-oriented – plan, not to mention a theory, administer political needs and investors' interests. Expedited urban growth at the global scale occurs without a concept – or with concepts from yesteryear. And that at a time when the planned city expansion areas are to become the *cathedrals* of the twenty-first century. We need new city centers of the highest spatial quality where we will enjoy spending time and which we will go out of our way to visit – like, for example, Salzburg's historic center. Let's take New York as an example: a simple grid with clearly defined public space, superimposed on site-specific conditions – for example, Broadway and the minimal urban design specification of a possible development of the parcels led to unexpectedly independent results: the only *modern* urban configuration that has thus far been brought about. Hence, simple principles and simple rules can yield quite complex and useful results.

That leads us to believe that all complex and highly appreciated buildings were brought about by way of simple basic structures and principles – and not by way of *form-giving*. City planning is, in other words, not a matter of defining building massing, but rather consists of rules, like a game of chess, that are open to the future and incomplete. To reconcile the two constituent components of the city – the memorable quality of the public realm and housing – we must begin to look at questions about density and urbanity from a different angle.

By the way, it is not only city planning that has been lost to architects, but also, at the other end of the spectrum, furniture design – the *mobili* – in other words, establishing the large scale on the one hand, and movement at a small scale, on the other. What remains is the formulated and solitary individual object. Not a cruel twist of fate, because in the history of architecture the exemplary individual object is of immense significance.

1
"11 Zufällige Schlagworte," in: Architekturforum Tirol (ed.): *Josef Lackner*, Anton Pustet Publishing, Salzburg, n.d. (2003), 234.
2
Interview with Hermann Czech conducted by Matthias Dusini, in: *Falter* 16/2004, 14.

IV

Layering and stacking

Studying structural conditions for the generation of form and space is one of our central and motivating activities. By employing different forms of manipulation, we bring about sensible frameworks – with this term we refer to systems that are serviceable for the respective function – that can be coded as identity-fostering buildings: the space or the form becomes special in some way and as a result recognizable and unambiguous. Identity, in combination with genuineness, is a key to appreciating something, whether a building or a city is at issue.

Superimposing two elements or structures in *layers* – such as old and new, public and private space – can, when they are kept in a suspenseful relationship, or in one of mutual respect, lead to the enrichment of their characteristics: the whole is greater than the sum of the parts – like in the song "The Jungle Line" on the album *The Hissing of Summer Lawns*, the melody layer of Joni Mitchell's iridescent song, developed from the underlying staccato, hovers above the bubbling rhythms of Burundi's martial drummer in a strange, oblique tension

Stacking similar elements, but elements of different size leads – almost inevitably – to an independent, often arbitrary spatial configuration with unknown potential, similar to the stacks of lumber in what were once ubiquitous countryside woodyards: the wood had the same cross-section but different lengths, and the stack usually was flush on one end. When we were children, because they lacked a function, these random spaces were highly attractive and useful. In our project *The Town Musicians of Bremen*, the vertical arrangement of different apartment types illustrates the potential of stacking different elements: the vertical assemblage of these various, two-story apartment units results in a special configuration with a strong identity and formal expression.

Conversely, arrangements of similar elements can also yield interesting results, when the *interstitial* spaces in the

Exhibition spaces with different types of lighting – all of them natural – fit into each other and are stacked atop each other, in effect, like a Russian doll. This gives rise to differentiated spatial situations in the museum interior – which, because they are situated behind an inconspicuous envelope, are unseen from the exterior. Upon entering the museum via a bridge spanning sunken courtyards one gets a premonition of the building's inner workings.

Costantini Museum
Buenos Aires
1997

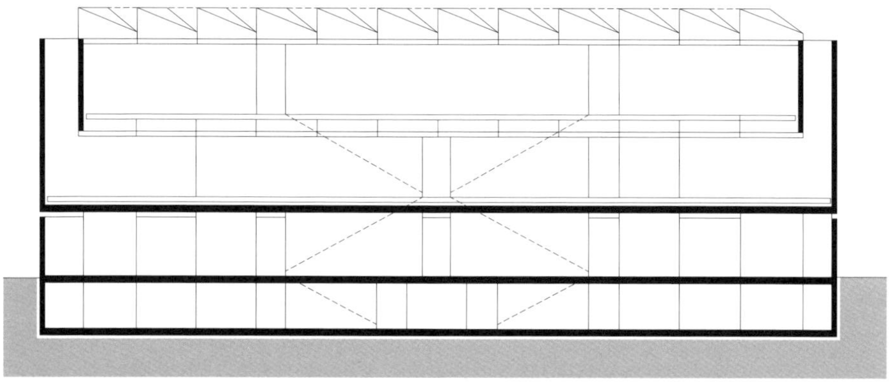

stacked structure are either unspecified or their use is left open to the individual residents. A process involving vertical or horizontal layering could, for example, be considered analogous to the Surrealists' *cadaver exquis*.

An outdoor swimming pool with accompanying infrastructure dating to the early twentieth century located in the dense assemblage of Graz's historic center was to be retained. Superimposed on the three-story building are new cell-like structures on piloti which add to the density of the existing building without encroaching on the courtyard. This new ensemble – linked by means of glazed bridges – is to serve as a residence for senior citizens. At the same time, the new parts of the building and the glazed spaces between them facilitate the installation of a roof above the historic facility and, as a result, allow it to be transformed into an indoor pool.

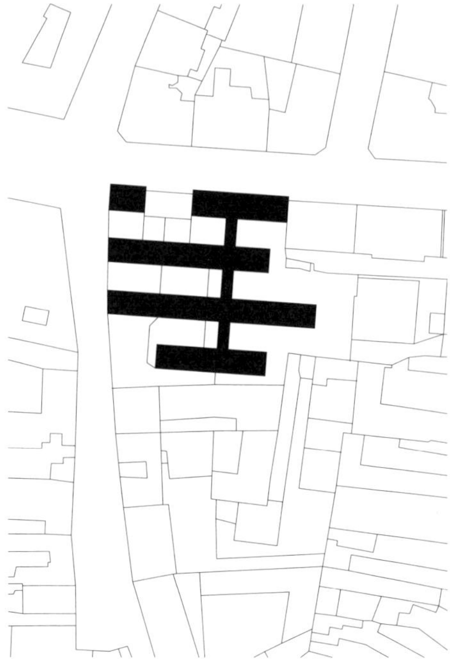

Bad zur Sonne
Graz
1997

The Organäists

In: *Was bleibt von der Grazer Schule?* Jovis, Berlin 2012

This title refers to a text by Helmut Richter in the journal *UM BAU* on the occasion of the publication of the bathroom he designed for S. Sares. In it he tells of the "structure of the aesthetic," which he finds in an "inventive ordering, testing and re-ordering of elements that are not characterized by belonging to certain classes or categories." Richter continues, "We try to at least do as little wrong as possible; when something is unsightly, it is in fact wrong." [1]

Helmut Richter's apartment building on Vienna's noisy Brunner Strasse is in many respects a pioneering achievement in social housing – and not only for Vienna.

Typology: an open exterior-corridor system that is shielded along the street by the plastically formed glazed facade. This system provides a daylit, semi-public, quasi-extension of street space as path to the apartment door and therefore allows a communication space deserving of the name to come into being.

Floor plan typology: a continuation of the so-called Vienna Block, an apartment building type possessing a central light well. Because the exterior corridors are positioned at a distance to the apartments, ensuring that sufficient daylight is available for the main rooms of the apartments to be oriented to it.

Technology: the frameless, 160-meter-long glazed facade is the first of its kind in Vienna. The construction method is a specifically modulated, reinforced steel frame. The very slender, space-saving exterior walls were clad in prefabricated, story-high wood elements with fiber-cement board sheathing on the outer face. The development of this prototype cut costs significantly.

Richter's buildings are always prototypical, always testing the limits of what is practicable and possible, which is what makes his work so compelling. Peter Cook calls it "hand-tailored tech."[2]

While there is something almost compulsively precise about how Helmut Richter conducts himself – there is no situation, no material, no detail that hasn't been fastidiously specified, nothing is left to chance – his former office partner Heidulf Gerngross is at the other end of the spectrum: here, chaos reigns. He focusses his attention on concepts, and his concepts are *patient*. His architectural conception is open; everything is in a state of flux.

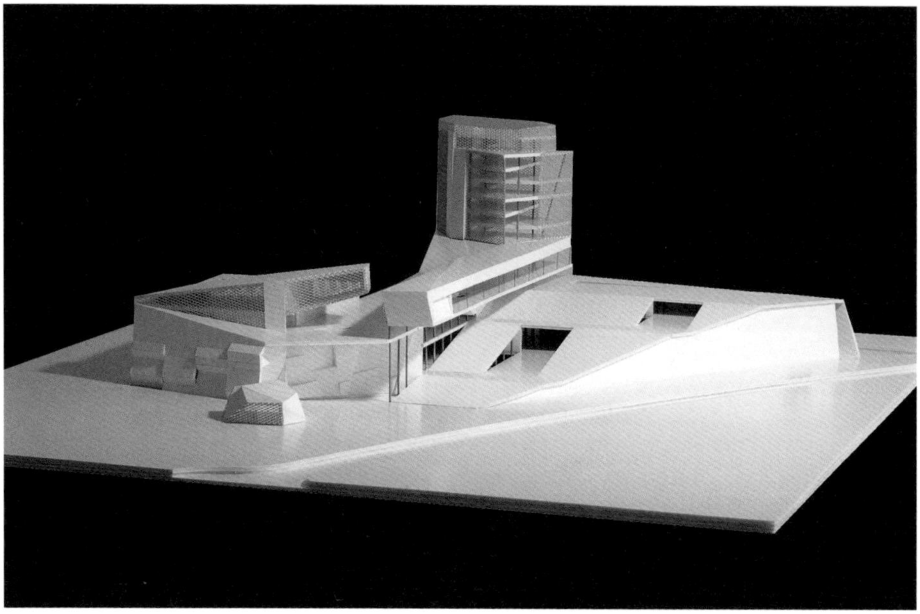

Salewa headquarters in Bolzano
Bolzano
2007

The new headquarters of Salewa, an outfitter of mountain climbers, is to be built on a prominent site at the southern edge of Bolzano – right on the *Autostrada del Sole*. Although the location is difficult urbanistically, a design of a building that is taller than the surroundings – with stacked-up functions – can make reference to the city center, as well as to dominant sights such as the Sigmundskron Castle. A layer of the terrain peeled away from the ground and raised up encloses storage areas and the garage and provides the aperture for a framed view of the highway. This newly formed landscape leads to a plateau with a view of the suburban development on Bolzano's north side and the agrarian landscape to the south. Access to the office zone and visitor area in the elevated "wing" and the screw-shaped tower rising up from it is had from this new brow of the hill.

The saying “to make a virtue of a necessity” could very well have been coined by Gerngross. He works in different areas of architecture, in a great variety of constellations, and he does not draw up plans. So he was obliged to invent the “plan of the spoken word,” with plenty of leeway for the inventions of his *amigos*. And yet: the *Gerngross framework* remains unmistakable – generous, unexpected, and thereby, stimulatingly fresh and unspent, yet pragmatic and, consequently, an unparalleled housing concept, because it's the others – the users, clients, etc. – who decide what is possible. He only determines the leeway, for he took leave of the detail years ago. “City planning is interior architecture,” is the way Gerngross puts it. His specific way of *sampling* with scales, and, of course, also with content, makes him unpredictable, but to an even greater degree, an ingenious architectural inventor.

The alliance between these two very special characters, which took the form of an architecture firm, was always a heady mix, so it's no surprise that they went their separate ways. And yet, it's impossible to think of one without thinking of the other.

1
Helmut Richter: “Bad S. Sares,” in: *UM BAU* 8 (December 1984), 77–78.
2
Peter Cook: Preface, in: *Helmut Richter – Bauten und Projekte / Buildings and Projects,* Basel – Boston – Berlin 2000, 6–7.

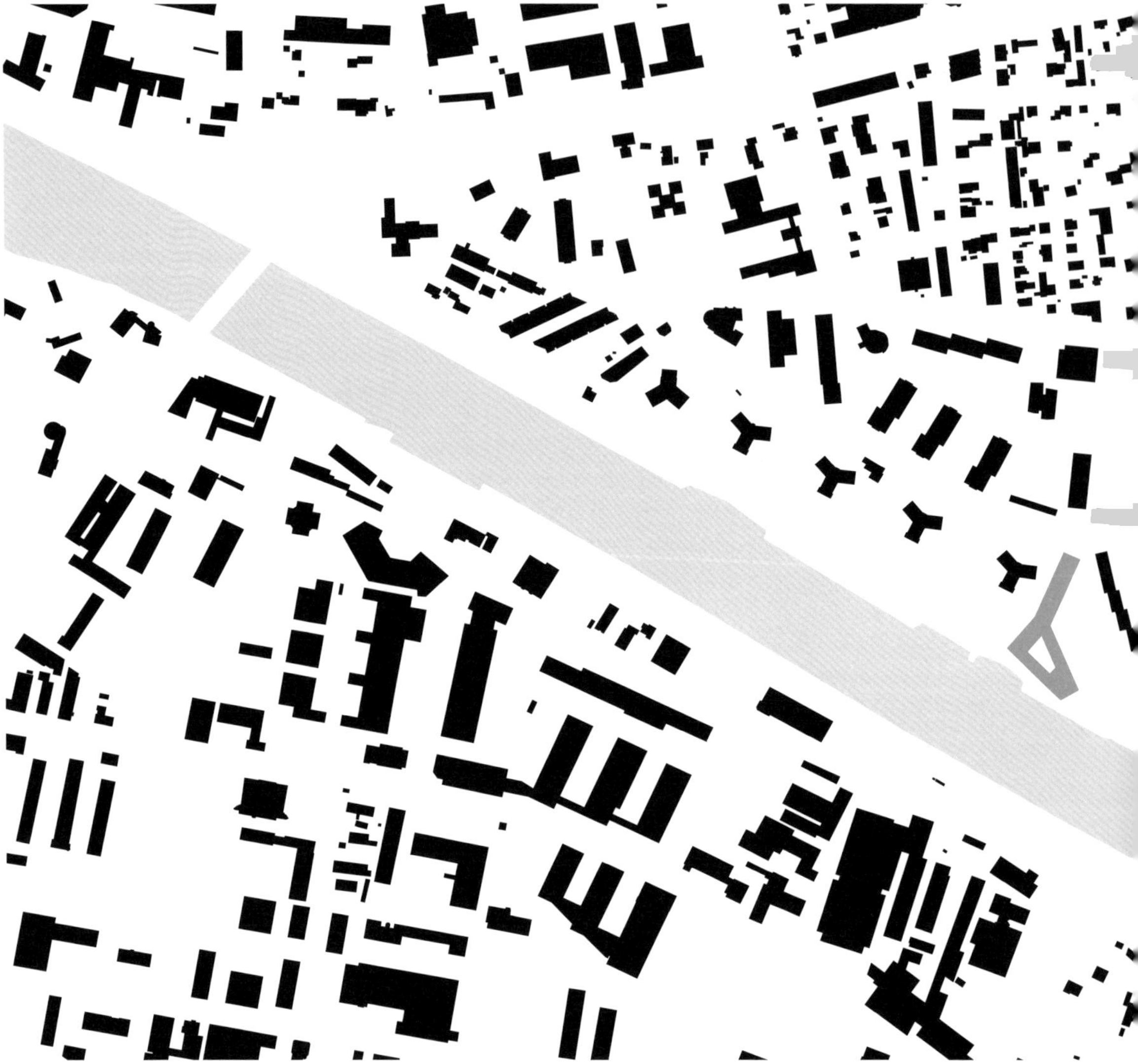

residence
Olympic Village
Innsbruck
2015

The building occupies a part of the riparian landscape along the river Inn. As compensation it shares its programmed spaces with the city's residents: the café – a place of communication – as a glazed volume in the park with both introverted and extroverted outdoor seating, and the chapel, a place of contemplation, a closed and sacred solitary structure, recognizable as such. The building massing suspended above these spaces and a square oriented to the river provide a datum line. The building is raised on piloti at the river bank, broken down into two- and four-story wings. This produces differentiated, generously dimensioned terraces for the residents. The general-purpose areas – with connections to the terraces, the park landscape, the Inn, as well as views to the mountains – lie on the respective ends of the residential floors. The transition from the public spaces in the building to the residents' rooms was articulated in different ways: a bench in front of the entrance to the room – bringing to mind the *benches flanking the area's traditional farmhouses* – create a discrete visual link to the respective rooms, thereby designating them private spaces.
The main entrance to the building is situated in the low-slung service wing. A multipurpose room on the ground level can be joined with the café to create a large event space.

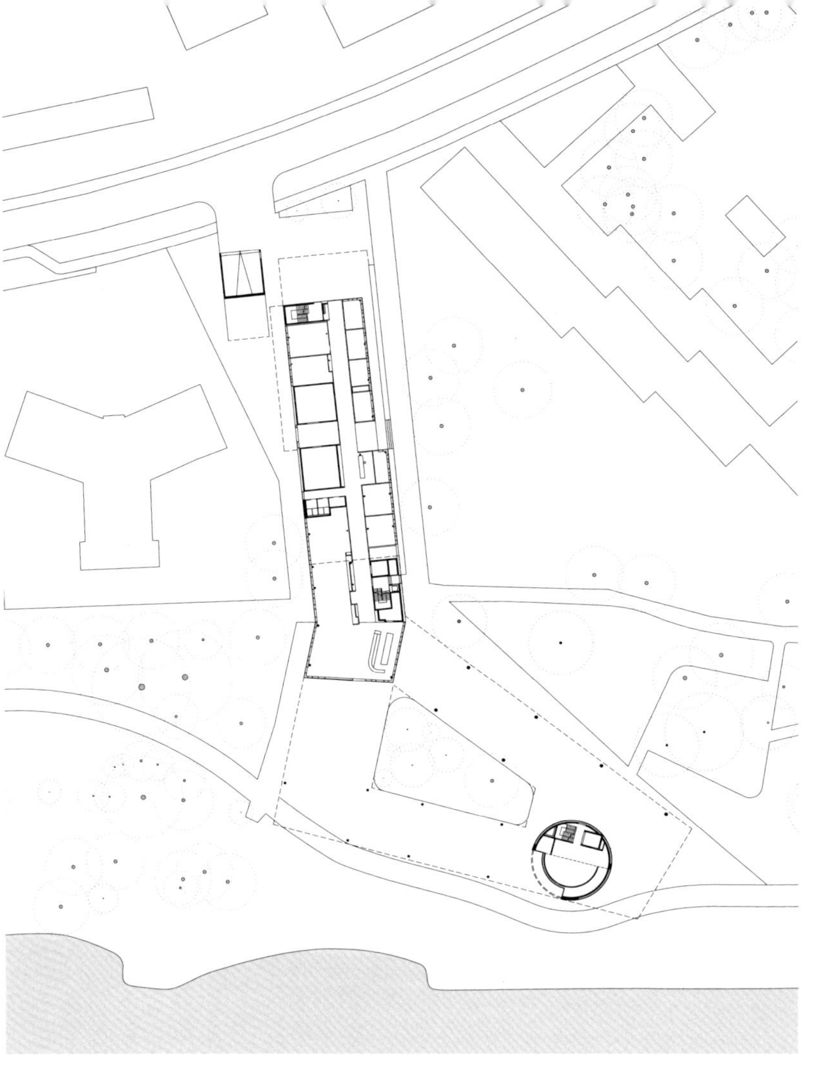

level 0

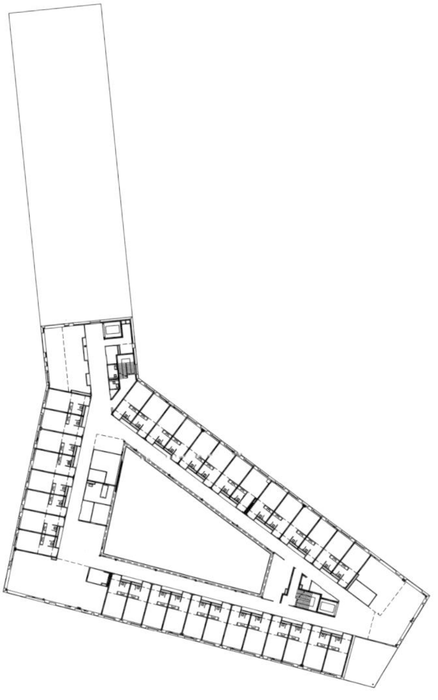

level 2

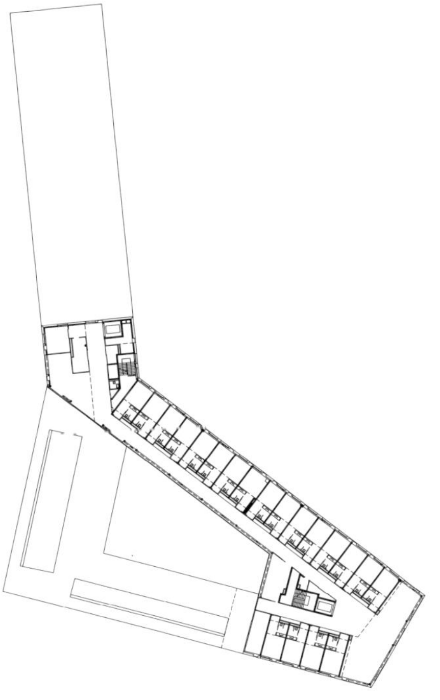

level 3

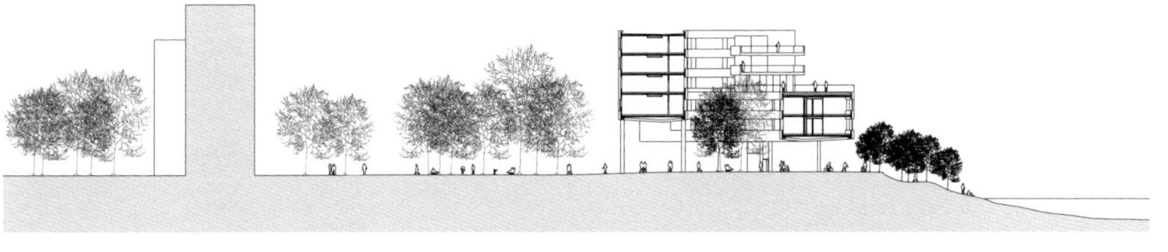

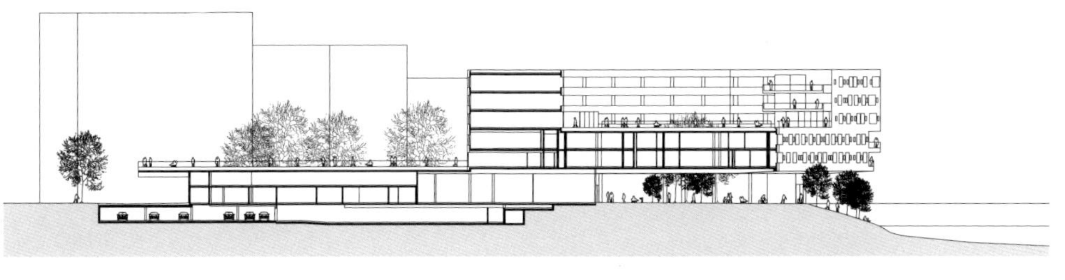

A gym as an eyecatcher for the general public is slid underneath the apartment building and extends across the entire courtyard. This creates a raised courtyard, for which we designed a garden. Access to the single-story units is had via an asymmetrically arranged corridor on every other story. The floor plans of the apartments are small in width, and extend either one or two axes. The apartments are oriented to the garden and to the west; they are fully glazed and have loggias along their entire fronts. On the upper levels are maisonette apartments and units that reach from the building's front to back.

apartment building
and gym on Hollgasse
Vienna
2003

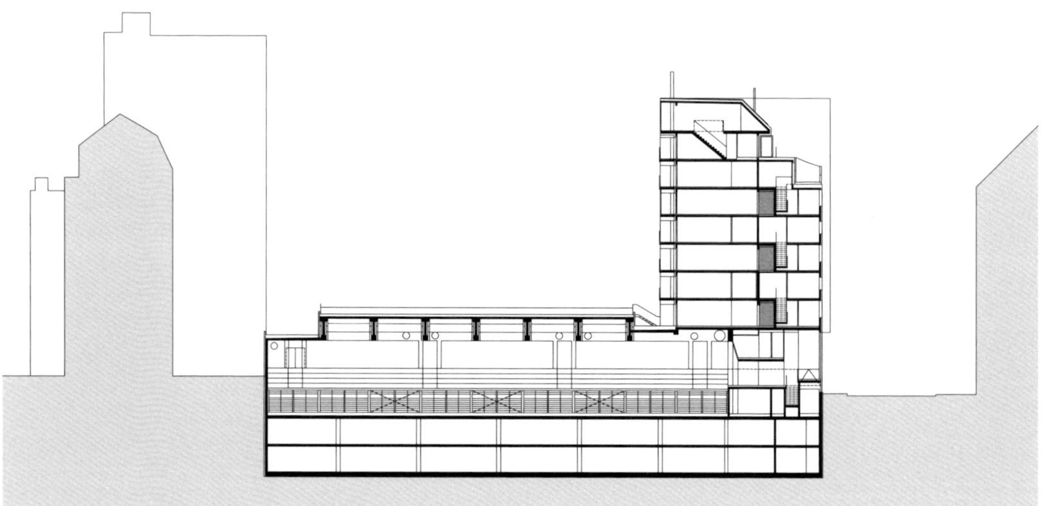

Zita Kern Space
Raasdorf
1998

Zita Kern is a farmer and a literary scholar. Fruit, vegetables, herbs, chicken, and cats make up one part of her idiosyncratic world, books the other. What was lacking was a bathroom and a space for writing and reading. The structure of the existing building provided the framework. An existing room with a wood-beam ceiling becomes the introverted bathroom; a few beams are removed to bring light in from above. The volume that has landed atop the existing structure is respectful of it: the new part functions autonomously and is poised atop the unaltered base. The massing, with a skin of cold-milled aluminum, absorbs the mood – of the weather and the surroundings: the skin makes the structure seem to dematerialize and obscures its purpose. In contrast to the existing structure, the new one more resembles a tent than a permanent dwelling. Though it is part of the farm ensemble, it is set apart from it. With simple means the intellectual sphere and the work of the farmer are drawn apart.

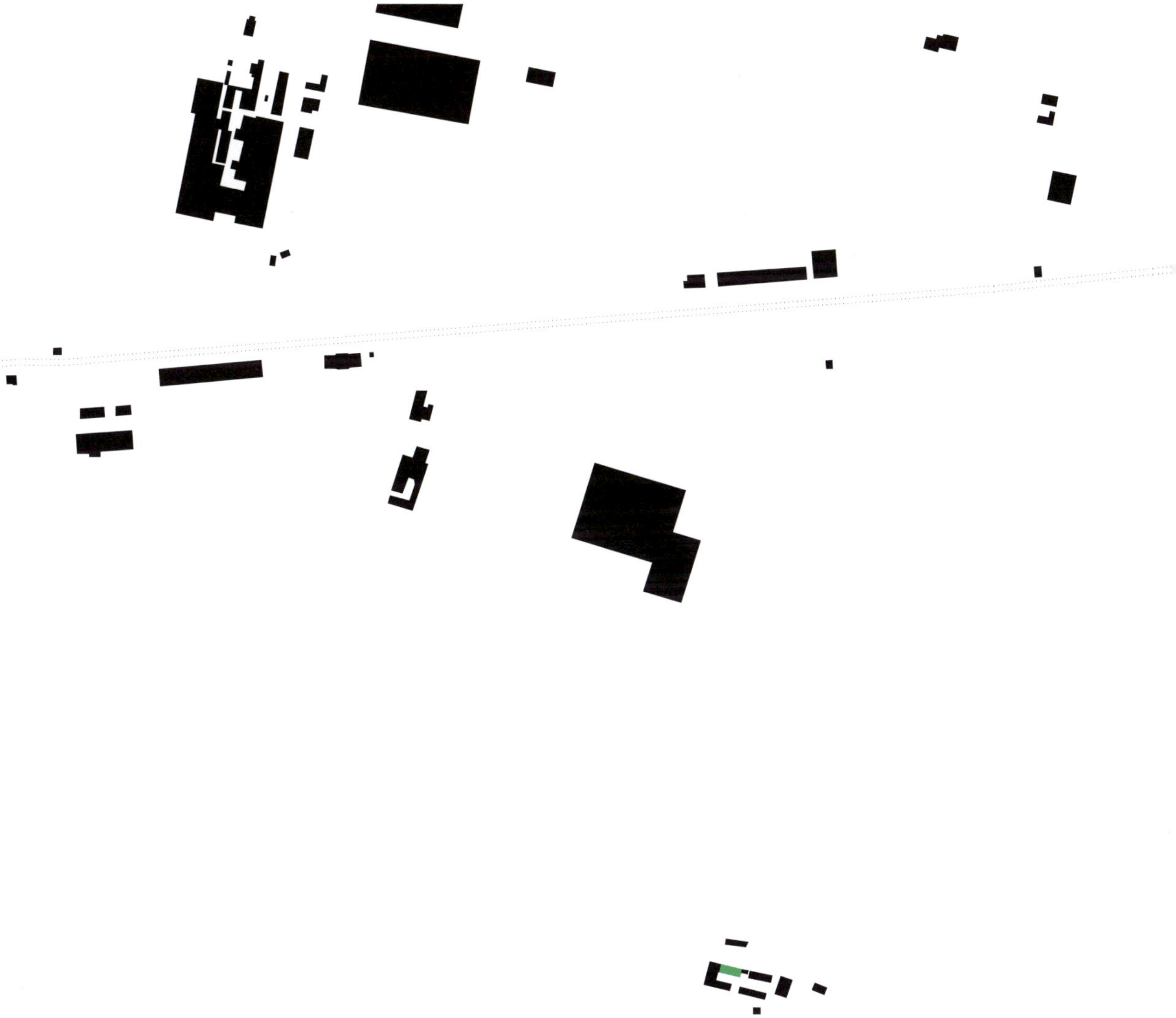

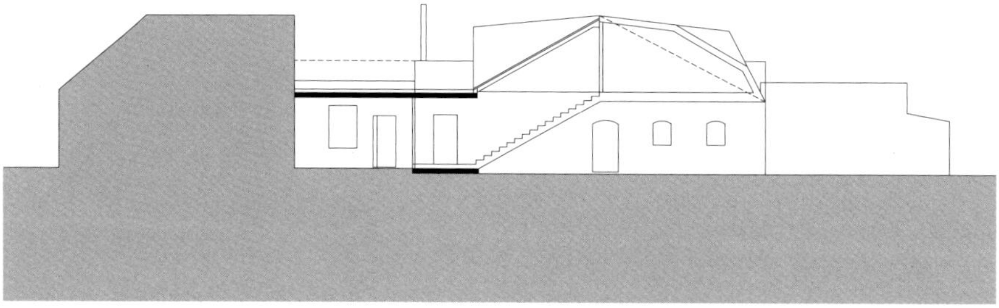

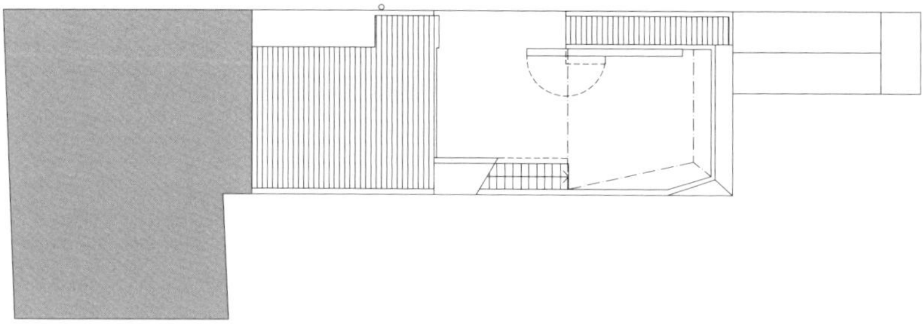

level 1

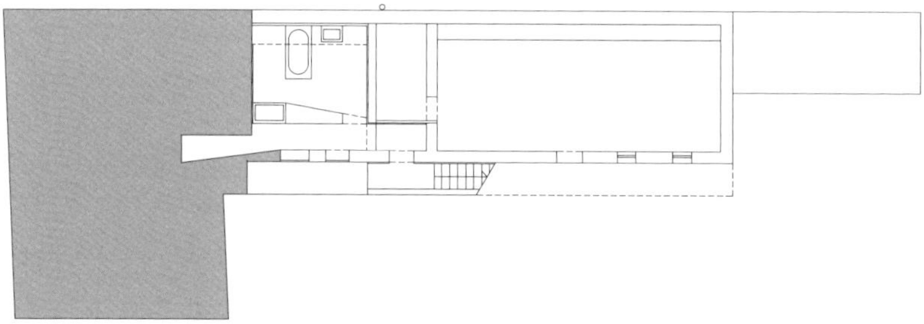

level 0

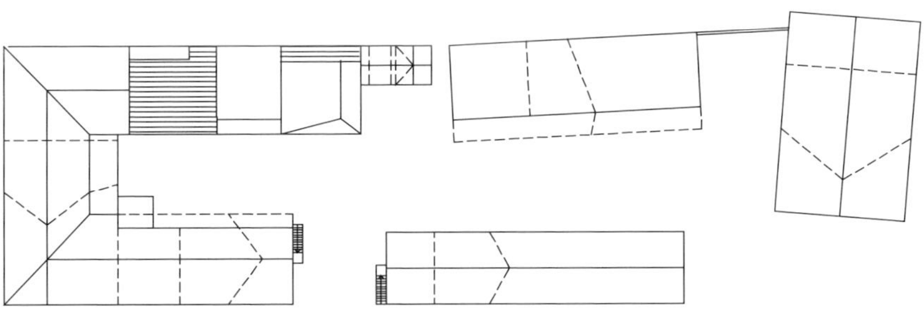

The building, which dates to the nineteenth century, was retained and a two-story addition was placed atop it. A lighting slit above the cornice separates the two parts. The upper level of the addition is set back on all sides, and there are terraces on three sides. A stair integrated in the volume leads from the lower roof terrace to a smaller viewing terrace at the very top. Both terraces are shielded visually from the street below.

apartment building on Bergmannstrasse, renovation and addition
Bregenz
2018

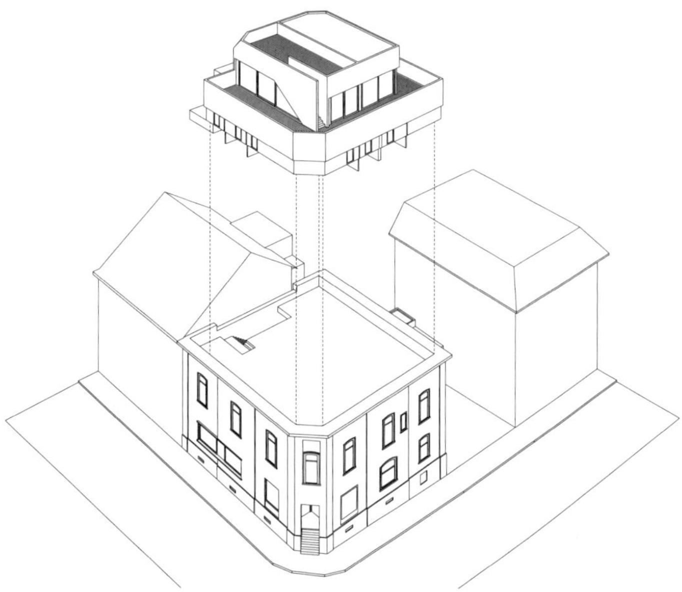

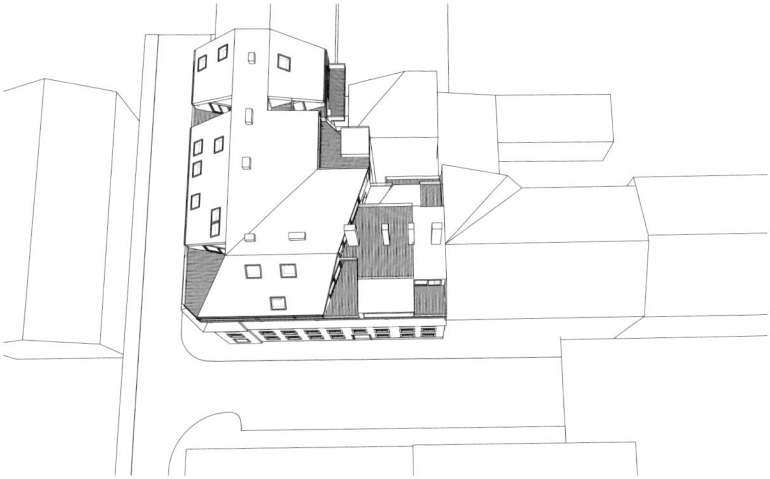

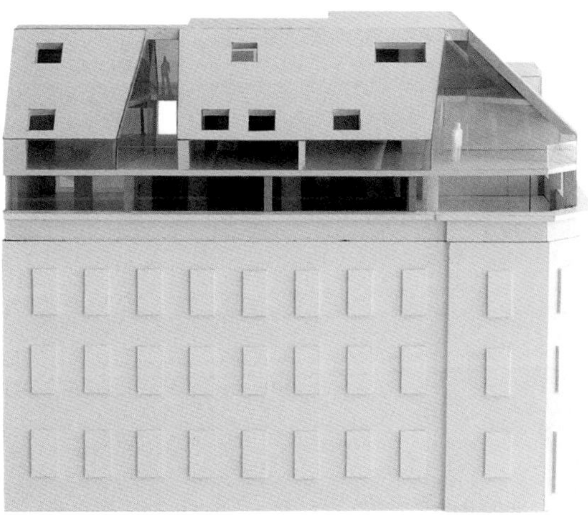

attic addition
Grangasse
Vienna
2018

Three new stories were placed on top of a three-story corner building dating to the *Gründerzeit*. Taking the allowable envelope as point of departure – as specified by the building code – by making cutouts and leaving parts unbuilt, we developed a framework for distinctive apartments and a diffuse silhouette. Consequently, on the top two levels are two-story freestanding *houses* accompanied by a continuous garden; a two-story apartment with a corner window; and additional distinctively cut apartments with large outdoor spaces.

apartment building
on Tokiostrasse,
The Town Musicians of Bremen
Vienna
2009

Borrowing from the Brothers Grimm story *The Town Musicians of Bremen* in which a rooster, a cat, a dog, and a donkey are stacked atop one another to create an *impressive* silhouette made up of banal elements, stacking up different apartment types is the concept guiding the design of this modified terraced housing. Different apartment types, each with a private outdoor space, are stacked up, producing a dense suburban package: below, an arcade space faces the street, and walled gardens face the courtyard. On the next level are maisonettes oriented toward an atrium, then rowhouses with terraces, and at the very top, allotment houses separated by courtyards. Single-story units with two-story loggias on Tokiostrasse *(Casablanca typology)* add to the variety of apartment types. This yielded sculpted building massing and fronting outdoor spaces. All units have cross-ventilation, and the kitchens and bathrooms receive daylight and can be ventilated naturally.

It is this spatial weave of different apartment types, with omissions at mid-height to make room for playgrounds and an all-purpose space for the residents, that gives rise not only to a social mix, but also to that very structural quality that is an essential component of urbanity.

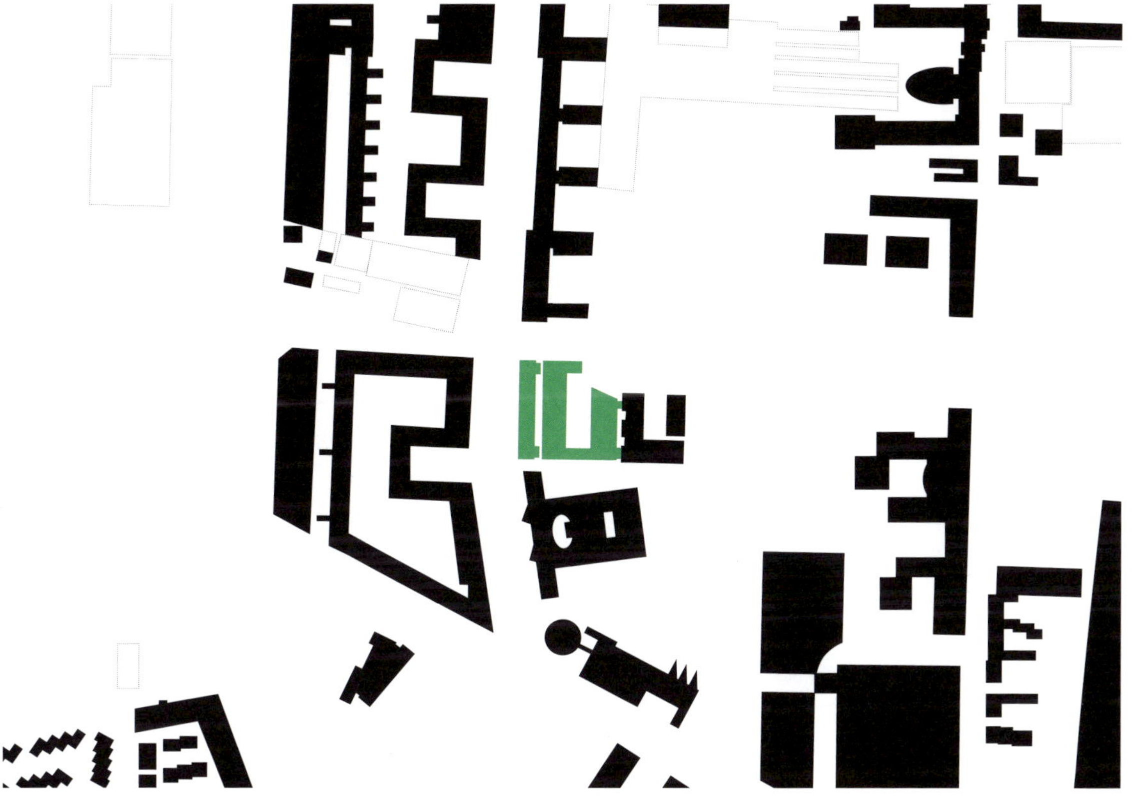

level 2

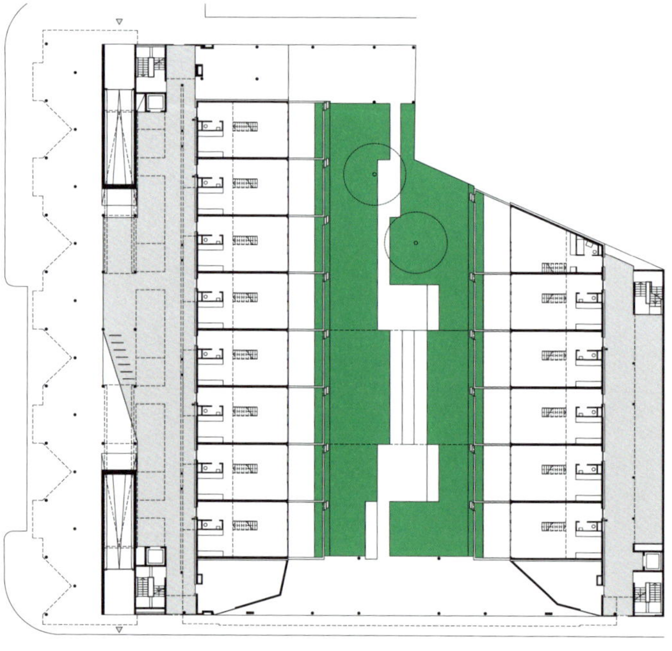

level 0

level 7

level 4

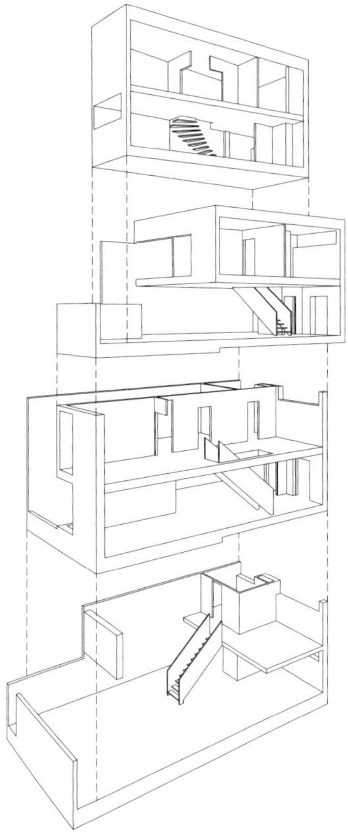

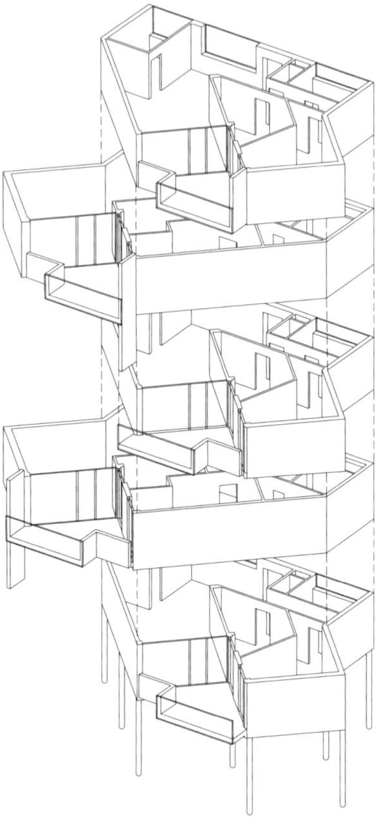

H
AUTOBUS
HALTESTELLE

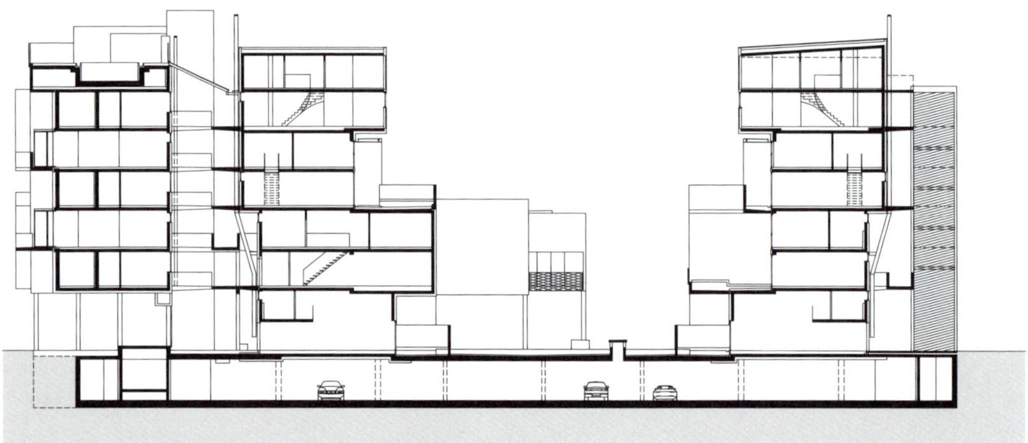

V

Fragmentary space and the Brancusi typology

Because the original idea – to set up a roller coaster for the duration of the exhibition – was not feasible within the available budget, we decided to build an abstraction, or, in other words, a fragment of a roller coaster half way up Graz's Schlossberg.
At the time we wrote: "One works for months at a time, but without reward. With the exception of the installation of some new luminaires with a neutral appearance, no improvements could be made to the infrastructure. And from the start, it had not been our aim to make changes to the overall structure. Some spoke in hushed voices of architectural visions – but bar any architecture. The question remains: how can one exhibit architecture if one doesn't exhibit architecture? Visions are ephemeral: therefore the damage is minor. There is no longer any mention of function. The architects were persuasive: robbed of their usual sphere of activity, they could muster only drivel. Exceptions are rare but noteworthy.
How things should be done – from the technical standpoint, regarding form and stance – has been formulated hundreds of times with much conviction. What remains to us is to ascertain: We cannot accept a division between architecture and what is typically referred to as life. Neurotic forms and emotional plague mechanisms must always be avoided. We do not conceal, nor have we ever concealed, the fact that we cannot believe that human existence can be satiated as long as biology, psychiatry, and education science are unable to take on the universal emotional plague and fight it just as ruthlessly as plague rats are fought. The purpose of architecture can be nothing else. Yet the term architecture has become a synonym for the strange illustrations on the comic pages."

Harter Laubfrosch (Tough Frog),
installation on Graz's Schlossberg
Graz
1984

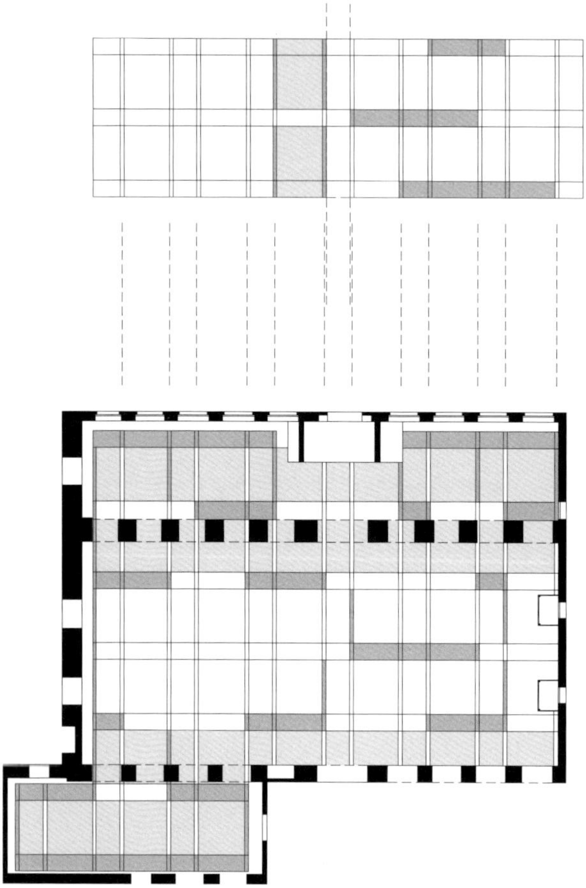

The Broken Mirror
Museumsquartier
Messepalast, Hall B – Kunsthalle
Vienna
1993

Using a system of wall elements, all of the same height – the ones running longitudinally have greater width, and crosswise, less width – a flexible and open exhibition installation was developed for the two separate exhibition spaces. By working this way we were able to unify the two different spaces – even though they are situated at a distance to one another, a connection is forged.

An arrangement of parallel walls of different lengths and positioning becomes interlocked with the surroundings, creating an inhabitable open sculpture in the existing landscape with spatial densification as one moves inward. For the realization, we specified bush-hammered in situ concrete and a roof structure of simple Corten steel beams with a glazed surface above.

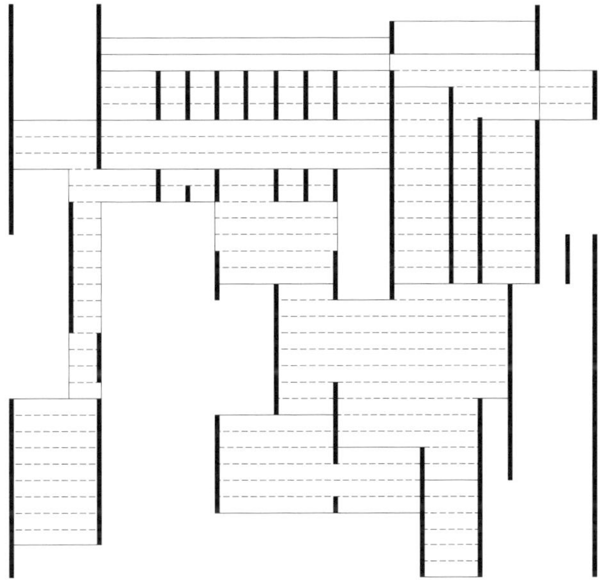

urn field
Linz
1999

Skanstes Street
Riga
2007

Riga's historic buildings are characterized by their marked three-dimensionality, which is based on simple geometric forms. Proceeding from there, we superimposed a pragmatic, high-performance basic grid with block widths of 18 or 29 meters and courtyards with a width of 40 meters on the site. One after another, parts were cut out of this maximum built density, until a specific, spatially differentiated concept that can accommodate the functions *came about*. This process rids the housing complex of its monumentality, and the separate volumes become legible. Strongly differentiating the heights of the buildings produces an indelible urban configuration that offers public areas that are staggered vertically, and support a mix of uses.

Today the issue of minimizing space while retaining a maximum degree of quality and spatial potential is, be it purely for economic reasons, one of the most important challenges in architecture. In particular, in connection with building in an urban context and the realization that density is only attractive in interplay with spatial openness and potential adaptability, and that density always raises questions about public space, what interests us is a methodology of omission – of the so-called fragmentation – as an urban strategy.

In our concepts we define only what we know – in housing, for example, that means, of course, the apartments – and leave everything else open: the necessary *gaps* in a structure. These gaps are that sort of potential that can secure the appropriation and, in turn, the liveliness of the public space. The process remains open, the structure always a fragment: nevertheless, a recognizable approach, a holistic concept, must always be perceptible.

Our interest in typologies – not only for housing – is, on the one hand, a result of our continued involvement with architecture competitions, but, on the other hand, the work invested in typologies is never lost, even when the competition is lost. We also use typologies as abstract design parameters that are used and elaborated upon time and again: for the single-story units with two-story loggias on Tokiostrasse we introduced the term *Casablanca typology* – named after the apartment buildings that two different teams – George Candili/Shadrach Woods and André M. Studer/Jean Jentsch – built in the nineteen-fifties in Casablanca/Morocco as a continuation of Le Corbusier's Unité in Marseille.

For us, the *Brancusi typology* – named after the artist's *Endless Column* – designates a building structure *in section* that, within a pronounced yet, in principle, simple building form allows for a free development of the inner workings. This typology provides for a special way of

Spark, feasibility study
Bratislava
2009

For the city of Bratislava we devised master plans in which we determined the urban planning parameters for a city expansion comprising some 50 000 apartments. A concept foreseeing three-story structures with identical cross-sections is superimposed on the site and, in keeping with the local zoning laws with respect to daylighting and avoidance of problematic corner situations, was layered to become a permeable and loosely distributed urban configuration.

level 2

level 1

level 0

level 5

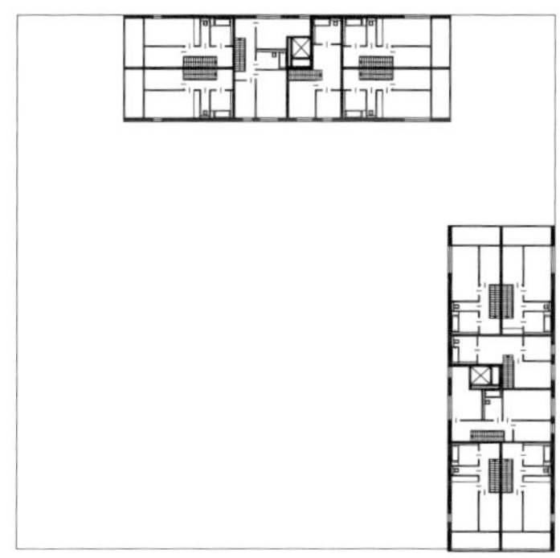

level 8

level 4

level 7

level 3

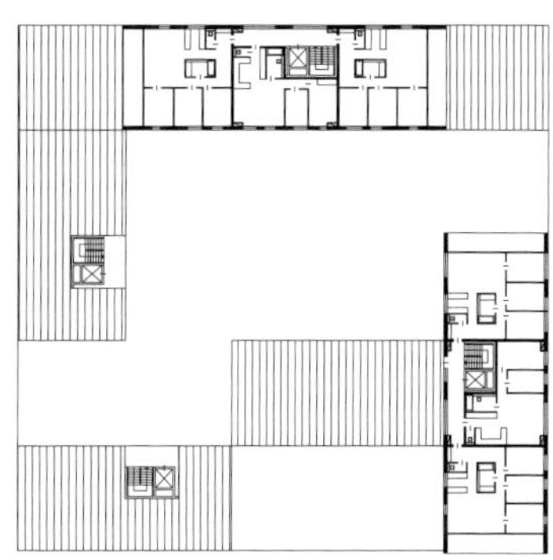

level 6

apartment building on
Alxingerstrasse
Vienna
2004

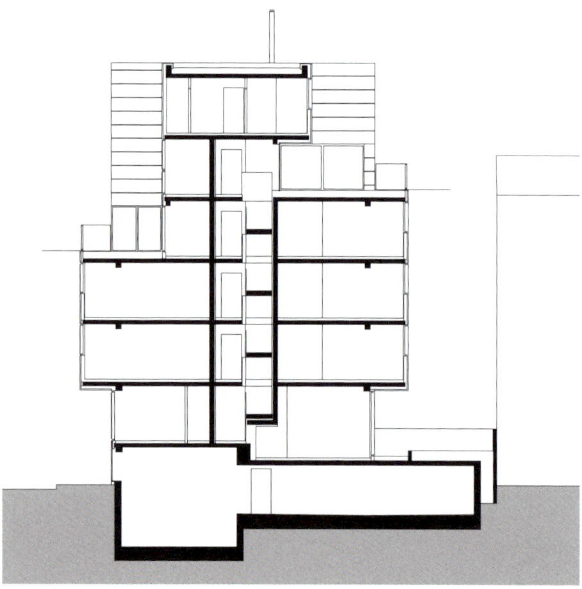

A collage of cuboid building components dissolves the *Gründerzeit* building fabric and, at the same time, forms a transition from the taller building to the shorter one: the three-dimensional shaping of the building in floor plan and in the vertical axis makes it possible to assign roof terraces to apartments from the third floor upwards.

A total of 11 of 14 apartments extend the entire width of the building, making cross-ventilation possible. The three remaining units are efficiency apartments. The sloped site is used to the advantage of the apartments on the lowest level: they have a ceiling height of up to 4.50 meters.

conducting light through a non-vertical facade, and can be applied at different scales and in different building typologies: from the exterior it is a repetitive arrangement of volumes, and inside there are a variety of spatial formations and facade forms

But the adoption of a *found* form also makes sense, because this opens up potential in a new context through its systemization of the form-finding process and cuts down on the occasional arbitrary decisions that are often difficult to negotiate in a shared design process.

Situating the building's circulation system at the center fragments the building massing and puts the stairway in a spatial relationship to the street heading toward it. The apartment types change as the building rises. Loggias of differing widths projecting out from the elevation toward the street – some extending to the building line, others stopping short of it – create private outdoor spaces large enough to accommodate different functions. They also allow the outermost layer of the facade to stand out in high relief.

apartment building with
office space at Hundsturm
Vienna
2004

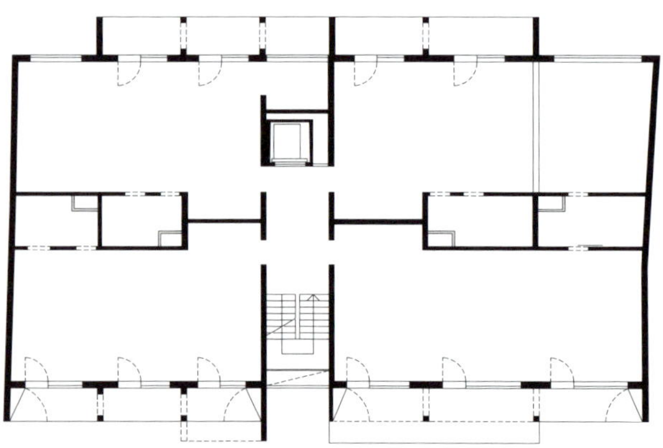

In: *Josef Lackner*
Architekturforum Tirol (ed.)
Anton Pustet Publishing,
Salzburg, n.d. (2003)

Architecture of the clear sort

Josef Lackner created buildings that added specific aspects to modernism's space-making project: with regard to re-defining and sounding out spatial possibilities of a simple geometrical silhouette, little exists that is comparable to his Ursuline school complex in Innsbruck.

What makes his architecture fascinating, and at the same time allows our work to profit from it, has to do with his approach – his way of designing was founded on a rigorous framework – a *concept:* every project adheres to its own set of instructions – and these are never used a second time. The process ties together the buildings and projects with their various, often unwieldy appearance to become one grand *oeuvre*. He developed his own logic for each project and submitted all further decisions – in some cases, with the exception of material selection – to these rules. This gave rise to buildings that did not adhere to formal wishes or obsessions, but rather whose appearances were generated by the respective concepts.

In this way, Lackner set himself apart from the process that was typical of his most prolific period, a process that was conceived of for repeated application and optimized for increased effect in drawing attention to oneself: style. Lackner's "style" is the concept itself, whereby completely different approaches may be possible depending on the task at hand, the site, and the problem to be addressed. As a consequence his oeuvre is multi-layered and multi-faceted, never slick or boring, but compelling, often surprising, and always decipherable and explainable. We like Lackner's idiosyncrasy – one might even call it bizarreness.

His *thing* is space; spatial components are defined and woven into a whole; nothing is residual. The appearance of the spatial configurations in their materialization is often irritating, sometimes difficult to decipher, and the person who takes interest is always rewarded with a wondrous interweavement, that allows an object that had been perceived as stand-offish to become an idiosyncratic yet matter-of-fact figure. A use-neutral envelope is never his theme; it's always about spatial quality – an invention as a response to a general problem.

At first glance, on account of their unwieldiness and inelegance, Lackner's buildings can be irritating, even shocking. Upon closer inspection it becomes clear that these are in fact built concepts that one can decipher and which then, at second glance, derive their beauty from their coherence. His buildings are the honest result of the underlying principle: an image arises that is at times almost shrill, sometimes

housing on Saalachstrasse
Salzburg
2017

Salzburg's periphery is characterized by heterogeneous fabric: without any transition whatsoever, large industrial structures border on neighborhoods with single-family homes. The low coefficient of density specified by the office of city planning (0.8) corresponds to two-story rowhouses. Our concept included, on the one hand, small, slender buildings that create a transition to the residential neighborhood, and, on the other, broad building massing in response to the dimensions of the area's industrial structures. We proposed two different apartment types: flats facing at least two directions and two-story units of different widths.

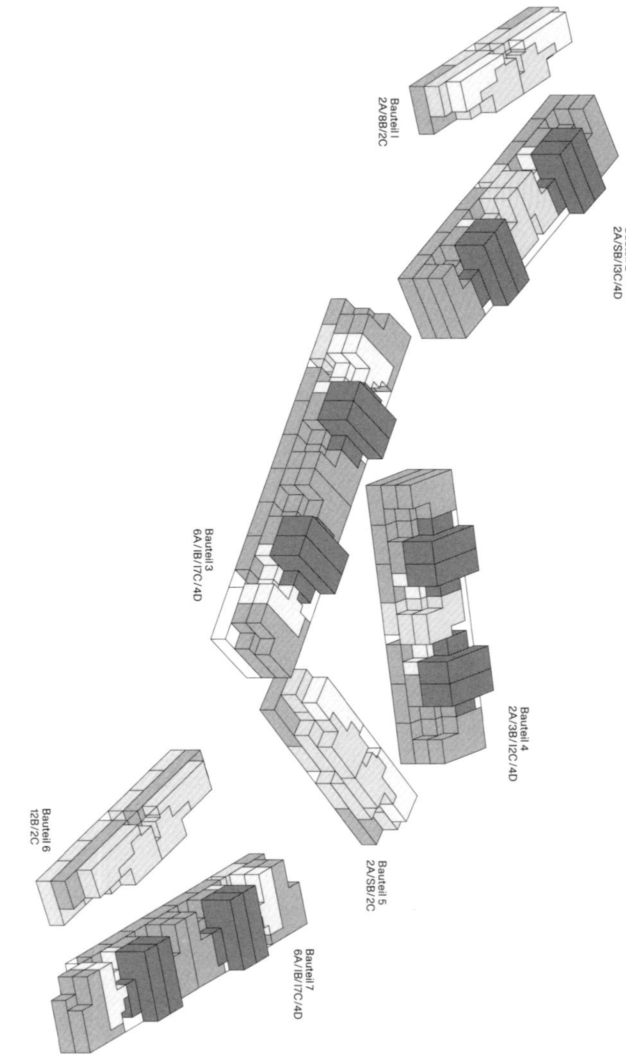

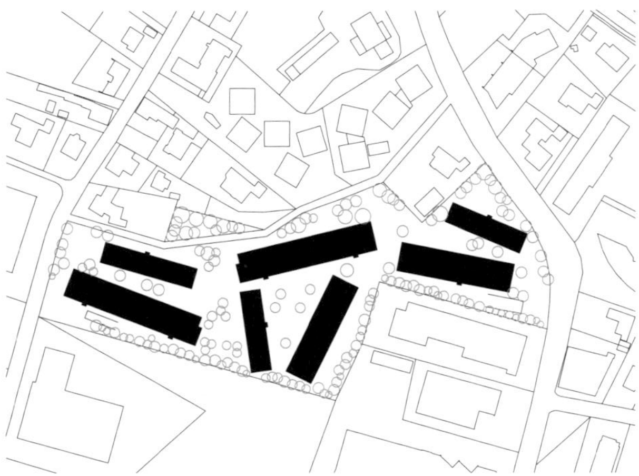

seems nonchalant and arbitrary, but that has arisen only through adherence to the project's foundational design rules.

The concept for a school grouped around an atrium, whose sequence of spaces is open throughout all levels, is fragmented by the context – the existing trees and the topography – and it is this fragmentation that shapes the school. This design process leads to a differentiated building form within the small-scale surrounding fabric and to an unusual significance of the building typology: it is respectful of the site's special characteristics and shows its reverence for the baroque city of Salzburg. The three-story atrium constitutes the center of the school; all of the major functional zones dock onto it. A *split-level concept* follows the hill's slope and makes possible half-story connections between the various groups of rooms, as well as a ramp system for universal accessibility.

school campus in Gnigl
Salzburg
2013

1

2

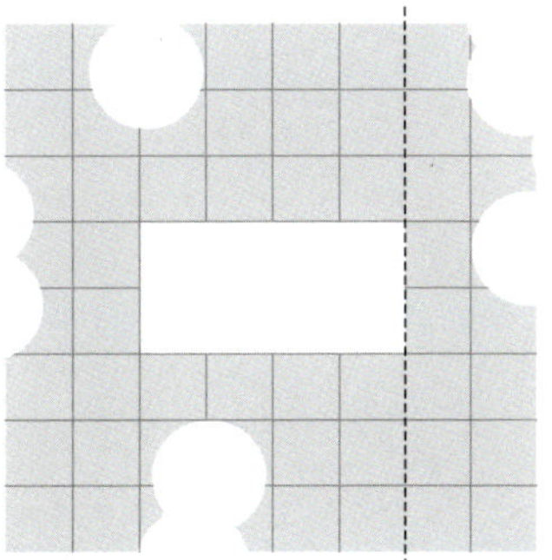

3

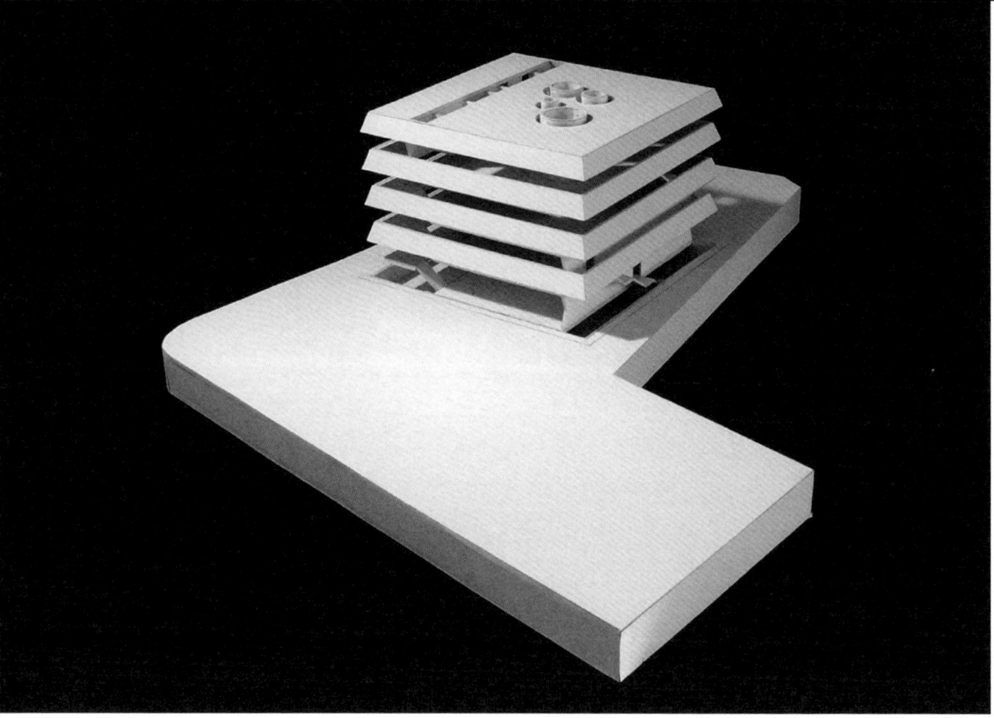

The building's structure results from stacking the functions. Lightwells of different sizes are cut into the complex volumes; they create distinct spatial atmospheres for the respective levels and in this way structure the building. The facade concept follows a principle in which direct sunlight is largely screened off, while leaving the view out to the surroundings intact. The *split-level concept* for the circulation links all of the levels and facilitates visual communication between them.

public library
Daegu Gosan
2012

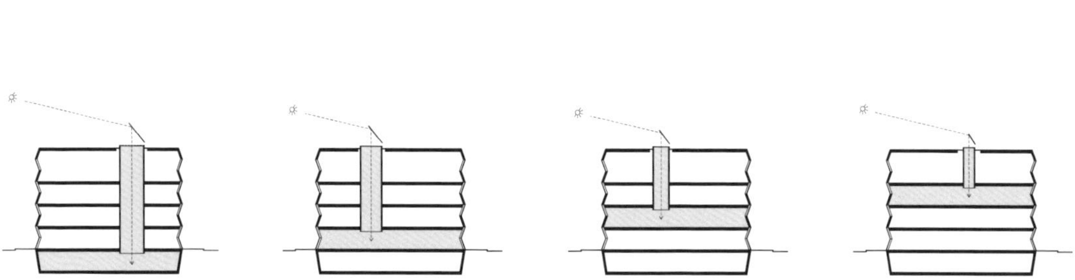

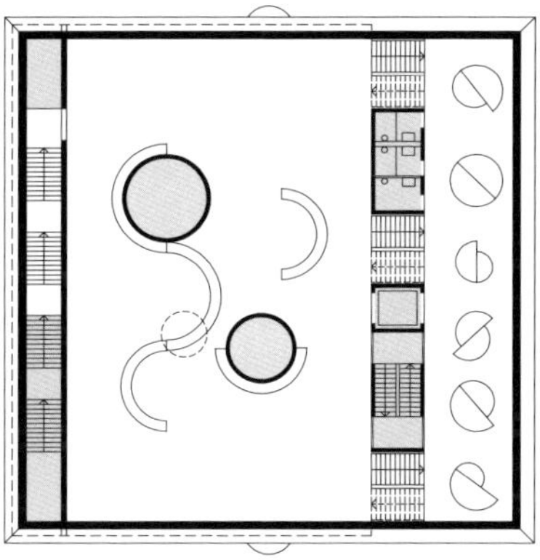

level 1

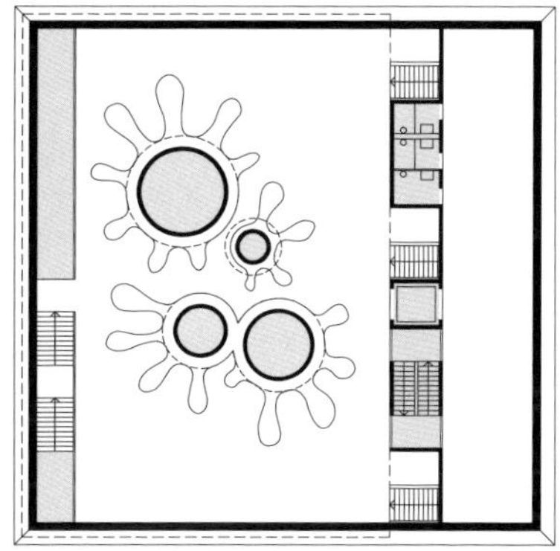

level 3

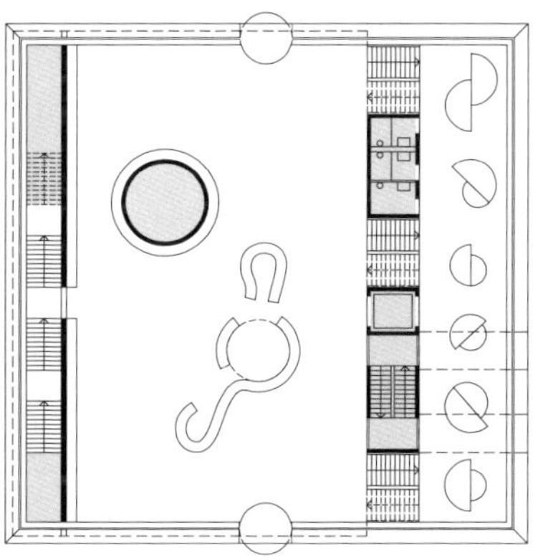

level 0

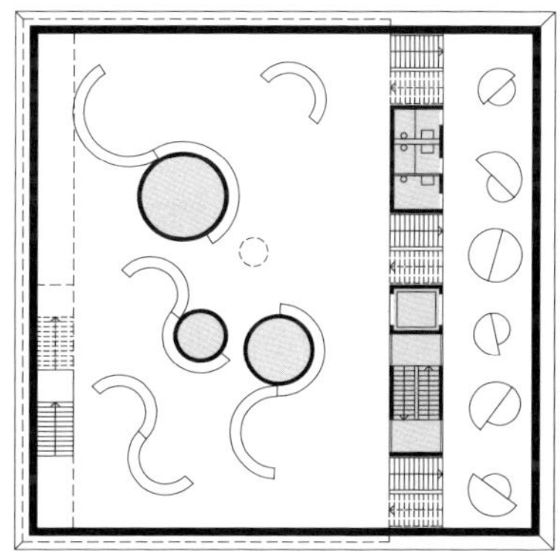

level 2

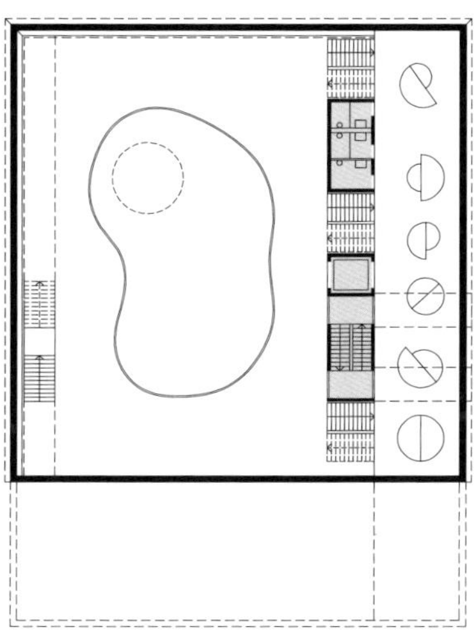

level -1

multi-generational housing at Mühlgrund
Vienna
2011

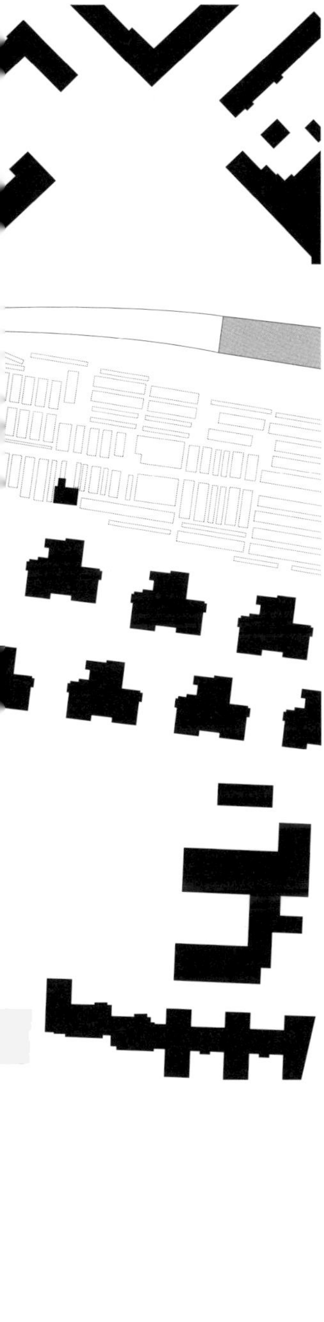

The location of the site – wedged in between the elevated rapid transit line to the north and suburban fabric to the south – led us to develop an exterior-corridor system at both ends of the building. A *coat* made of vertically faceted perforated metal cloaks the side facing the rapid transit line and the short ends, regulates the daylight, and provides views of the surroundings. This *metal coat* gives rise to a hall that is part of the building's thermal volume and offers special qualities: it is long, narrow, and tall, and is characterized by different light moods and varied spatial choreographies. A cascade stair in the slit between the circulation leading to the apartments and the metal wall leads from the main entrance, which is situated in the west, to the top floor. In between, planters were installed to create a vertical garden (Atelier Auböck + Kárász) that, with the help of tension cables, plays an important role in defining the space.

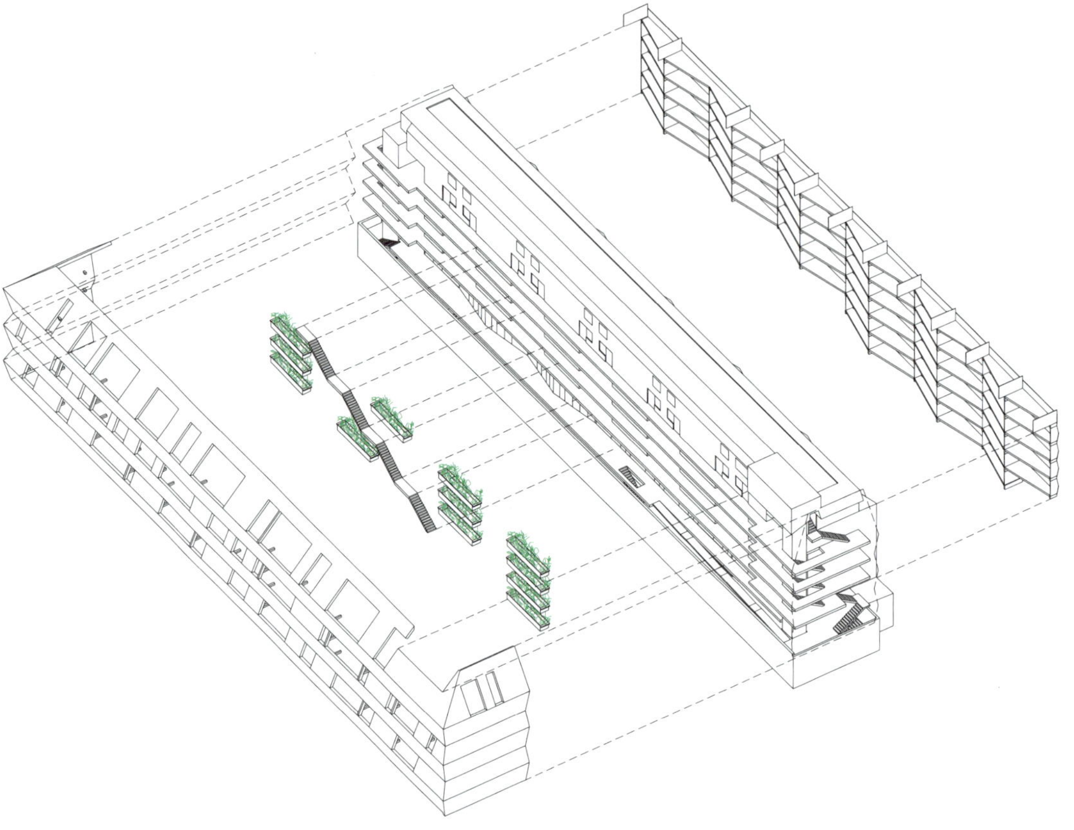

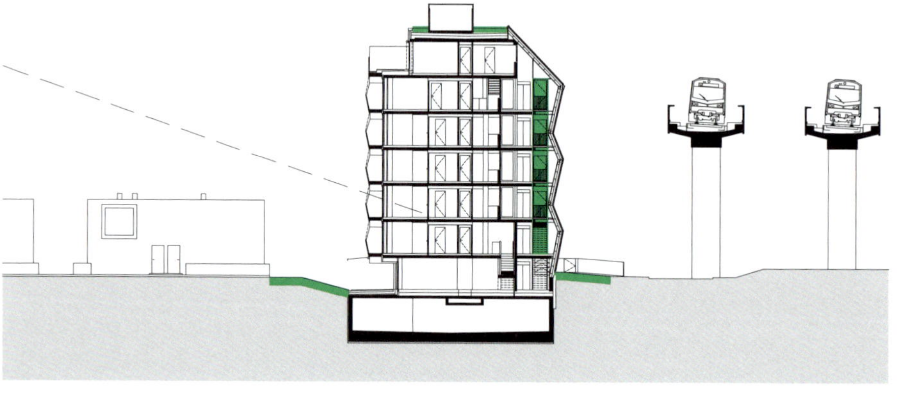

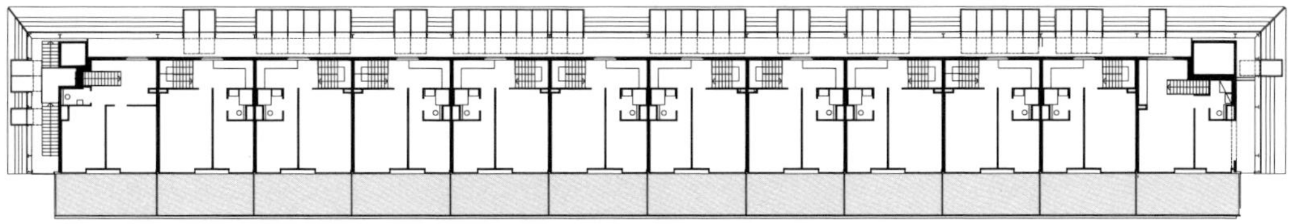

level 5

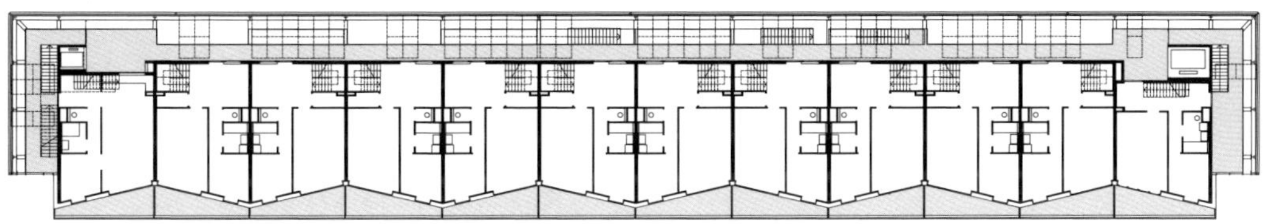

level 4

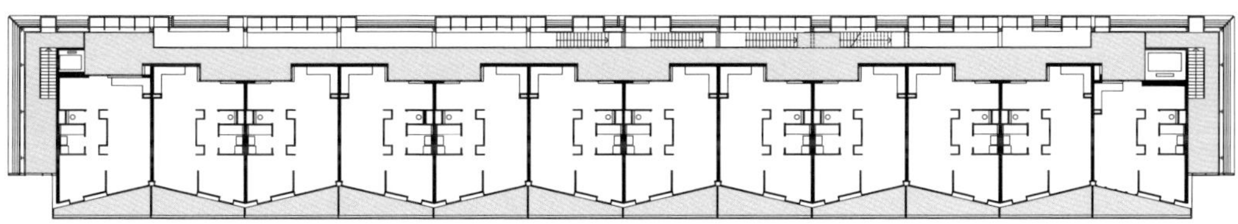

level 3

-70%

-70%

VI The context and the exception

The exception proves the rule. Although most of our projects are strongly characterized by abstract concepts and typologies, there are some that have come about by means of a topographical or contextual approach. Under certain conditions, interesting spatial innovations can arise in dialogue with the context: together, the existing building stock and the new *part* create a new whole, an architectural space that is more than the sum of its parts, whereby the interventions, seen individually, represent – in Franz West's sense of the word – an *adaptive*. Not until the two parts come together does the *meaning* come about – in other words, the architecture. The quality of the existing building stock and the reaction, *on equal footing*, of the new to it are the prerequisites. The context, on the other hand, can turn up in a great variety of outward appearances: the condition of the building, a special topography, or simply the lack of any identity whatsoever – in other words, the proverbial *greenfield sites* – can provide the occasion for specific spatial configurations.

pharmacy "Zum Löwen von Aspern"
Vienna
2003

The site is in Aspern's centuries-old core and borders two streets. Extending across the space like a *flying carpet* is a long-span reinforced concrete ceiling. Its ends curl up in a gesture to the adjoining streets. Inside the building, the walls and ceilings are made of cast-in-place concrete, while the ends were executed as prefabricated units. Courtyards structure the building massing. A large courtyard surrounding a chestnut tree faces a street; a small atrium with a newly planted gingko tree brings light into the pharmacy's main space. The salesroom is structured by *ribbons of light* that are flush with the concrete ceiling. Where they extend into the space, they metamorphose into shelves. A display garden with medicinal herbs and a roof terrace – open to both employees and visitors – round out the spatial offerings.

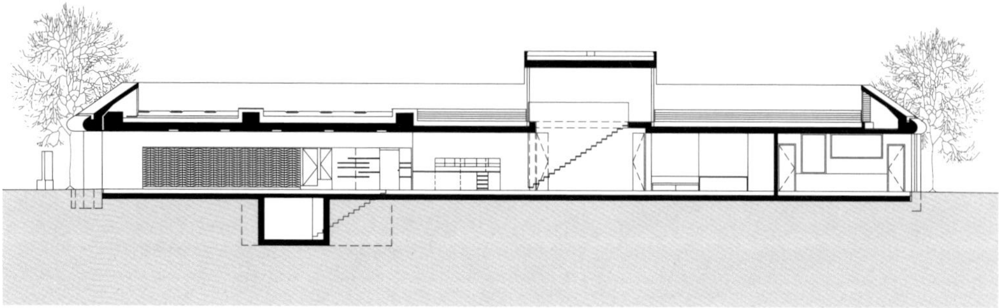

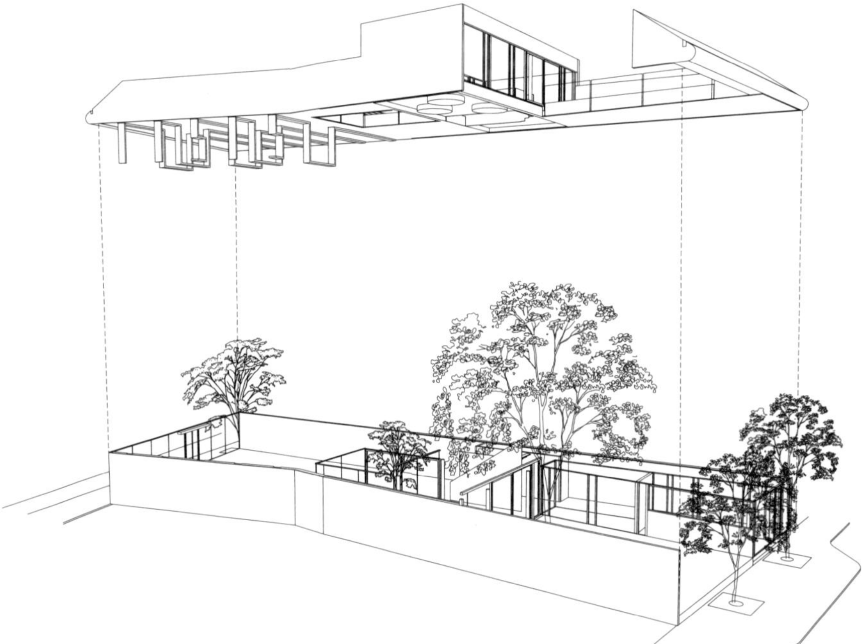

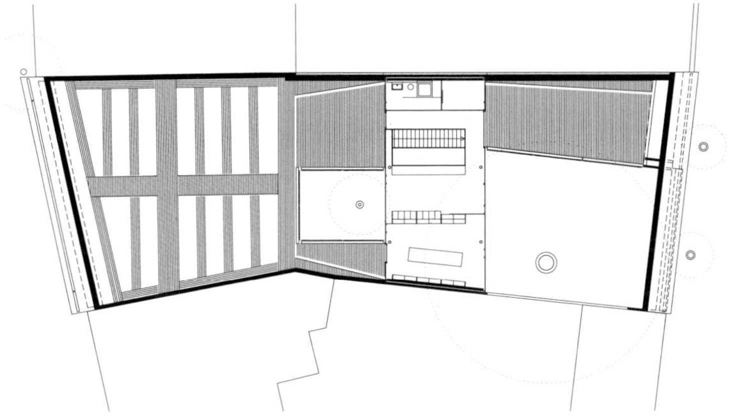

level 1

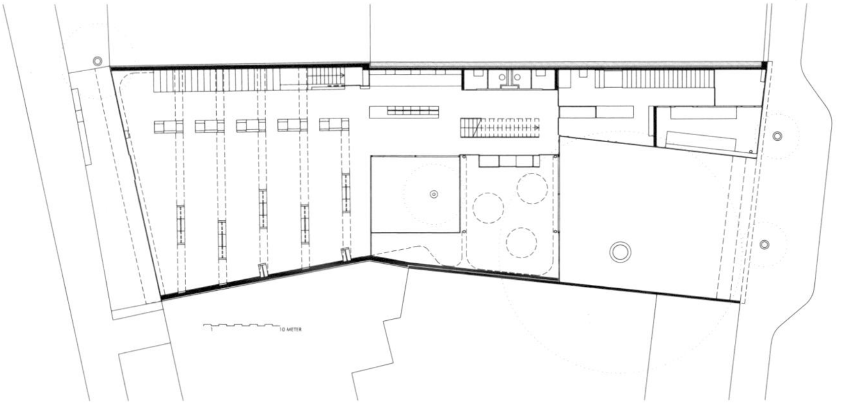

level 0

A P O T H E K E
SCHUHE MONIKA

K6, high-rise on Kundratstrasse
Vienna
2007

The zoning prescribed elliptical building massing. It stipulated a 70-meter longitudinal axis and a 26-meter cross axis. By working with glazed loggias staggered from floor to floor, we interpreted and shaped the structure three-dimensionally as a *residential tower.* The loggia mesh is like a *chain bracelet* slipped on the *high-rise* wrist. The two different ways the loggias are positioned determine the apartments' floor plans.

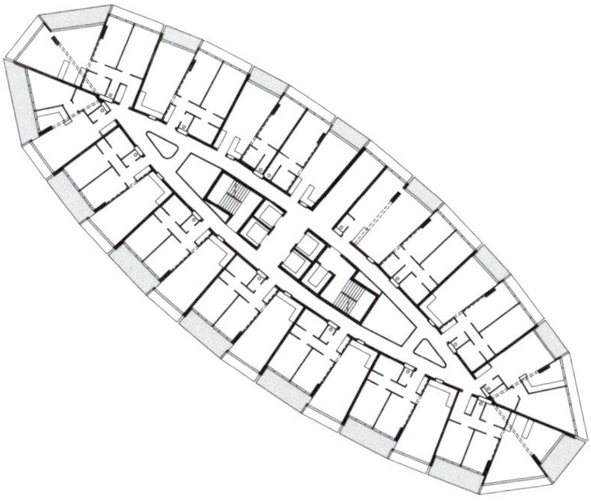

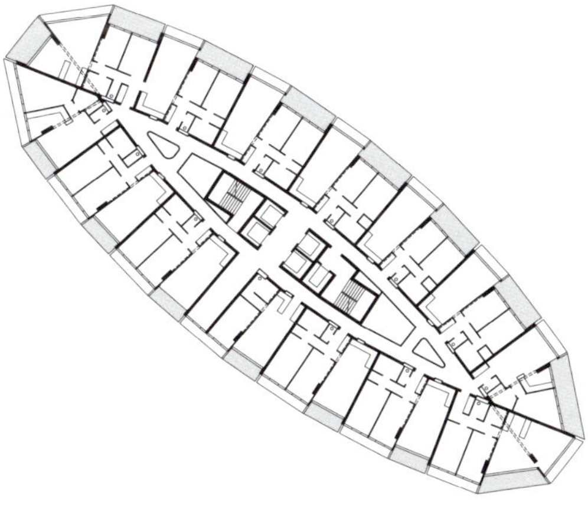

The site, which is bordered by a street on two sides, is occupied completely by the new building, whereby three garden courtyards in the west, each with spatial definition on three sides, and an atrium in the east are out of the massing. The main sequence of spaces lies along the north-south axis between the classrooms; it is structured by three different types of lighting. The rectangular part of the site hosts classrooms positioned at right angles to one another, while the gym and other shared spaces are situated in the triangular part facing the street.

school on Zehdengasse
Vienna
1996

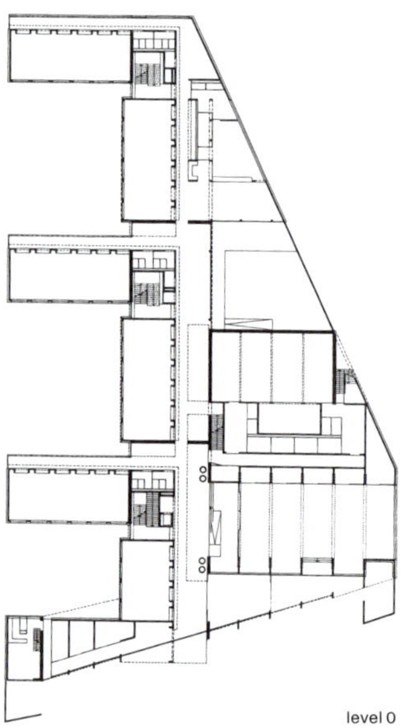

level 0

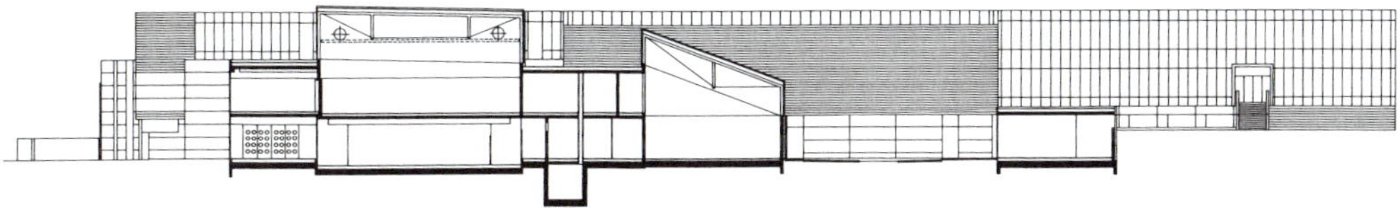

pre-school in Stadtpark
Vienna
2010

The concept foresees a double-height continuous space that offers a variety of spatial qualities to all the different classes. The aim is to create a spatial loop with hidden paths. Each class receives its own stair linking the two main levels. On the one hand, these stairs ("wormholes") structure the space (by creating niches), and are, on the other hand, part of the structural system. Airy, gently sloped main stairs are situated on the ends of the building and between the classroom zone and the playhouse. A special retreat – an "island" for the children – is created by the "interior terrace" atop the sanitary cores. Bridges from the gallery provide access to these retreats.

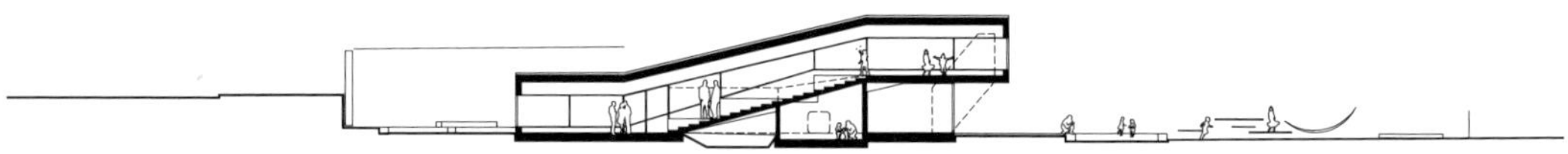

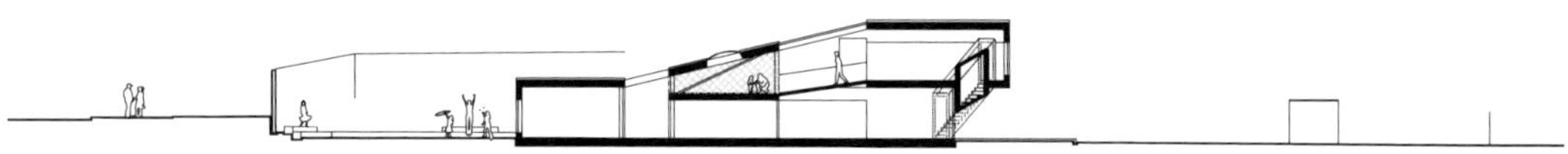

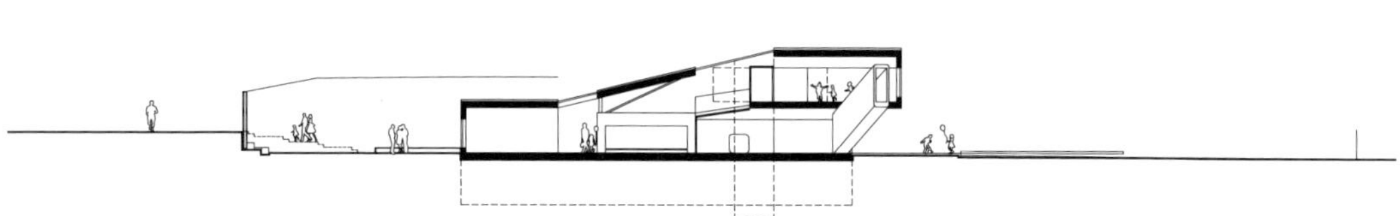

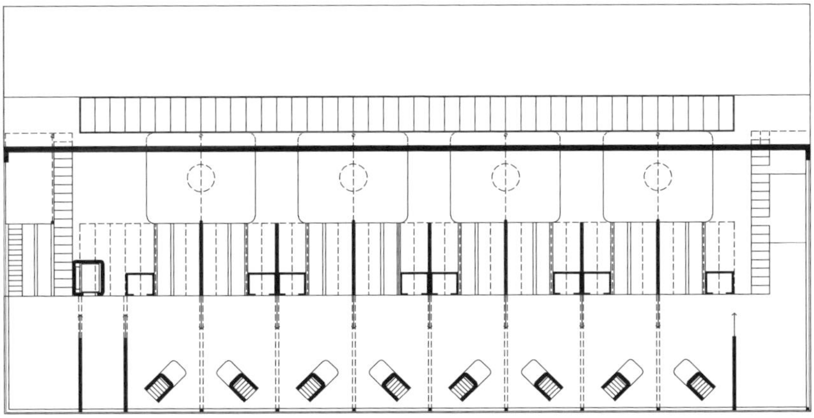

level 0

hospital entrance pavilion,
SMZ Süd
Vienna
2009

The pavilion is the information center on a hospital campus. In keeping with its function, its free form contrasts with the hospital's orthogonal system of free-standing buildings. The two-story structure can be entered on ground level from two sides and serves the general public. Round openings in the roof allow daylight into the main part of the building. One large opening in the ceiling above the ground floor directs daylight into the customer zone.

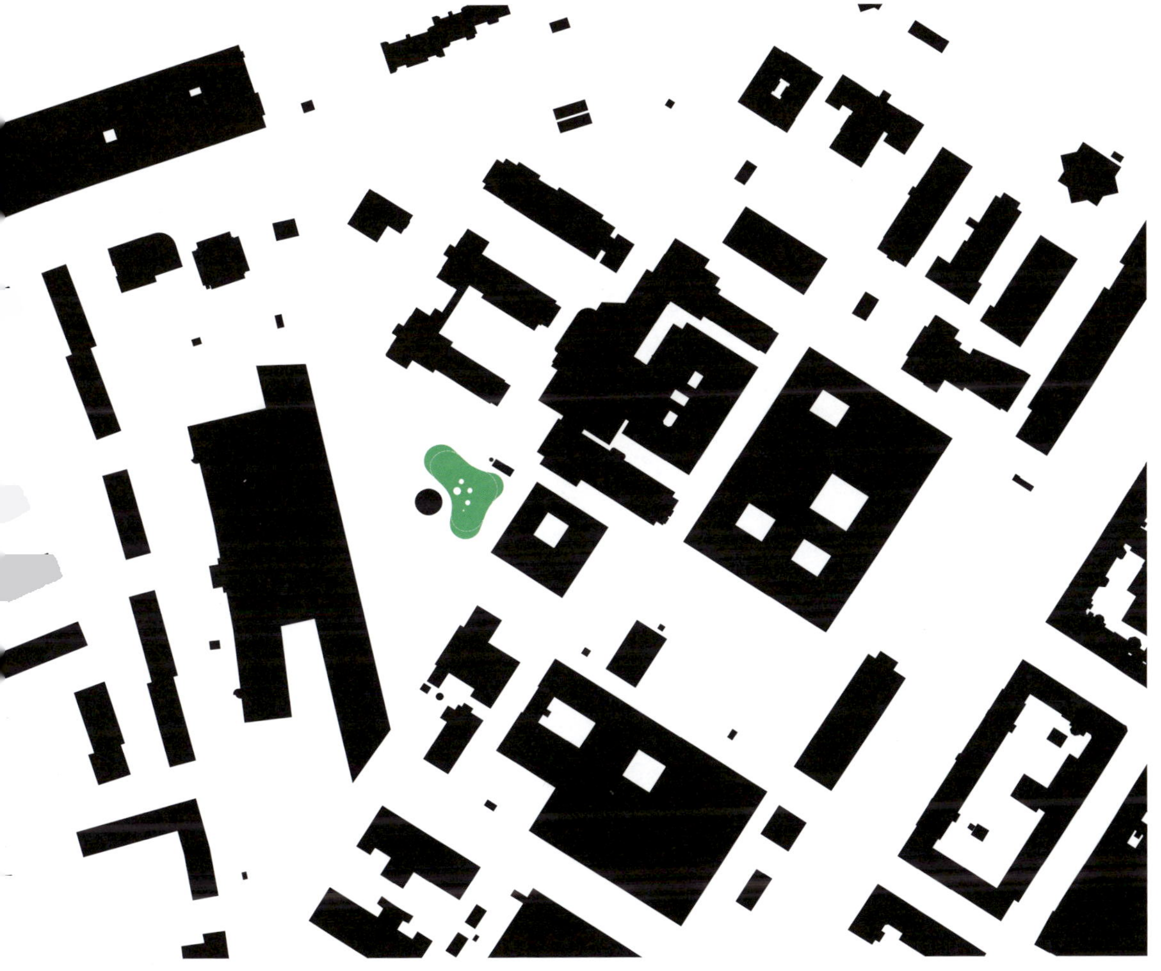

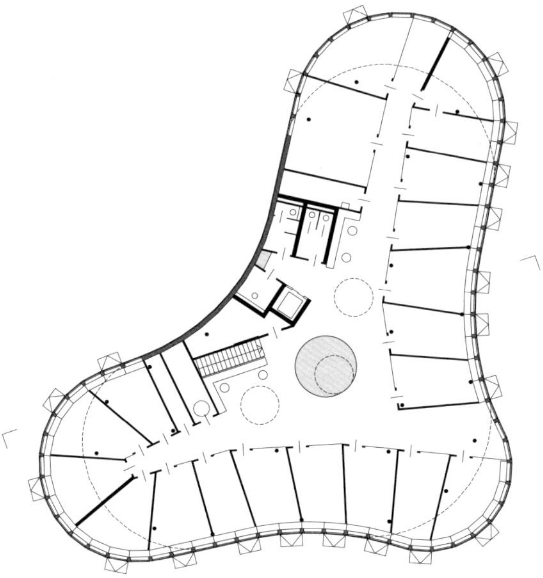

level 1

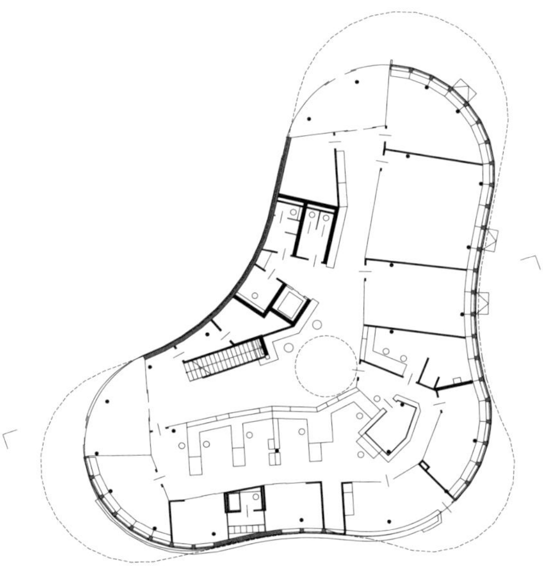

level 0

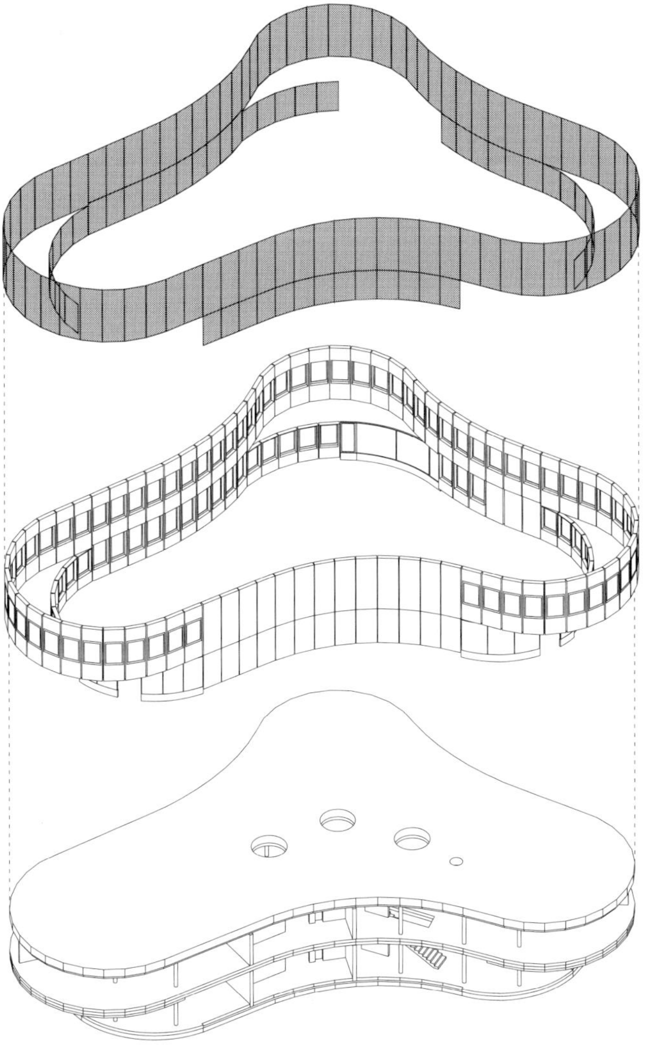

EFAFLEX
production facility
Baden
2004

The site is located in a business park. On account of the lack of built context, the building configuration was derived from its program: an office with a view on the upper level, a storage space on the ground floor. Raising the office zone requires a slightly more elaborate means of construction, but provides the opportunity to survey the operations and the well-lit spaces. The massing on the upper level shelters the entrance area below. The offices on the upper level are glazed floor-to-ceiling on three sides. Skylights above the stairs and the break room allow additional light to enter the heart of the office zone. The activity and the production in the main hall can be surveyed from a window in the office. The building is sheathed in a matt, metallic panel skin.

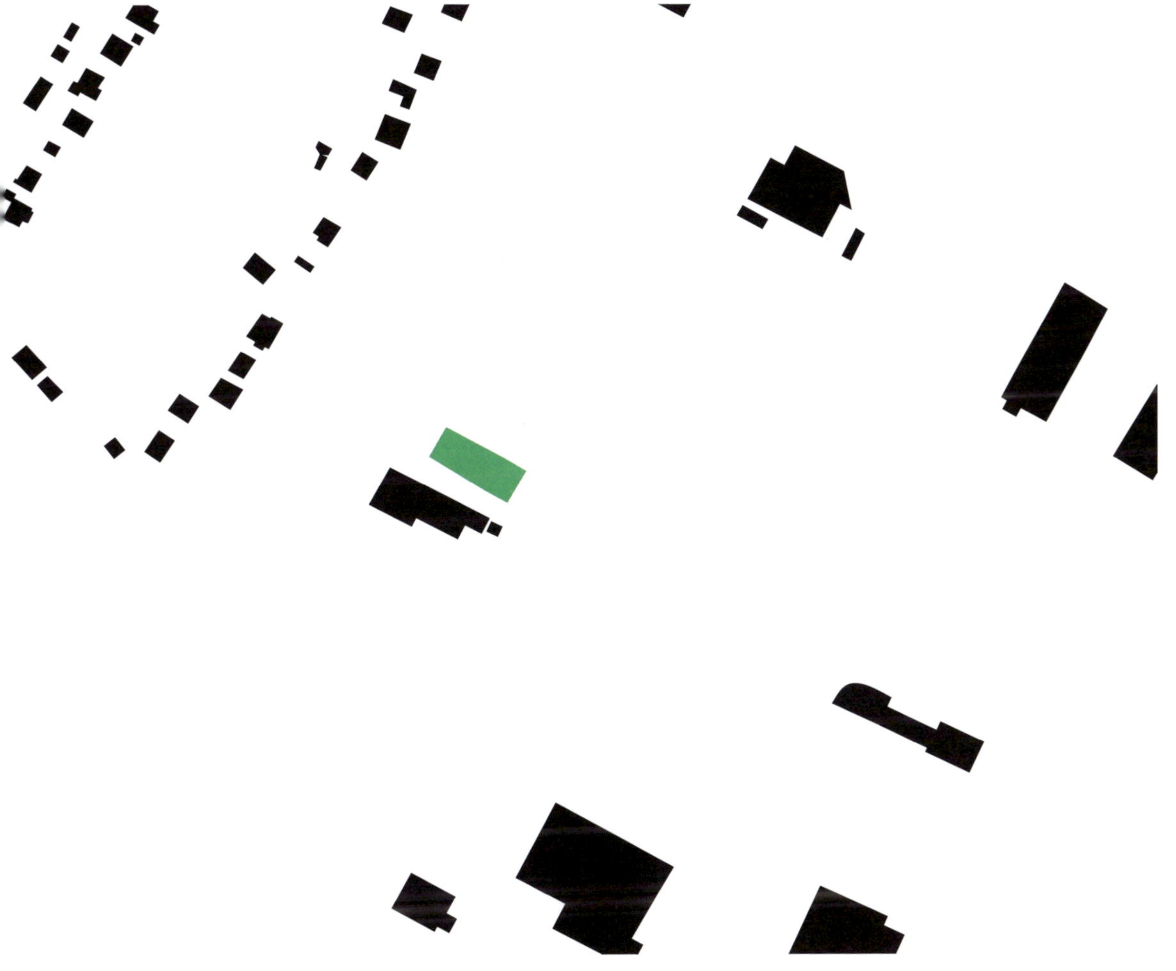

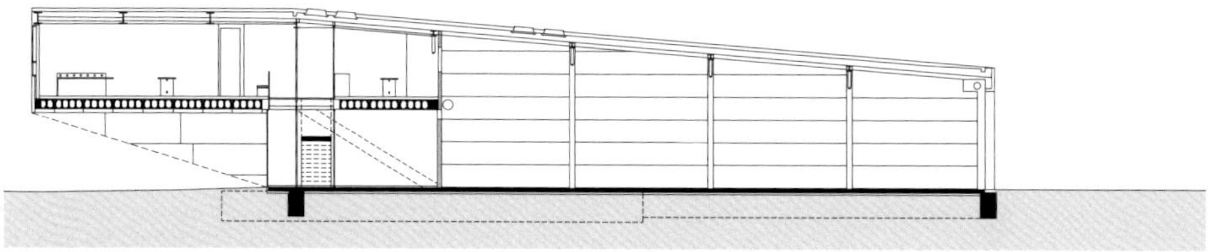

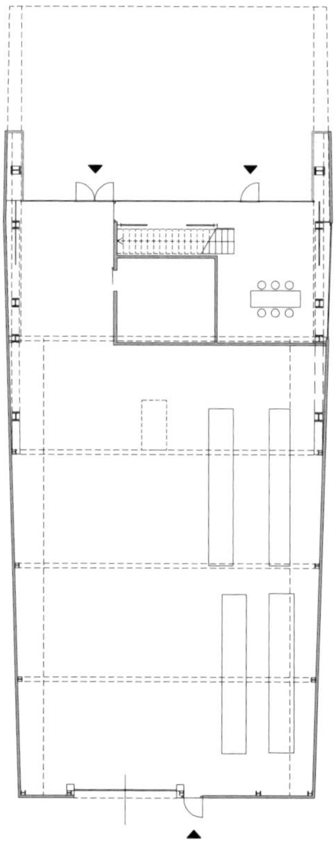

level 0

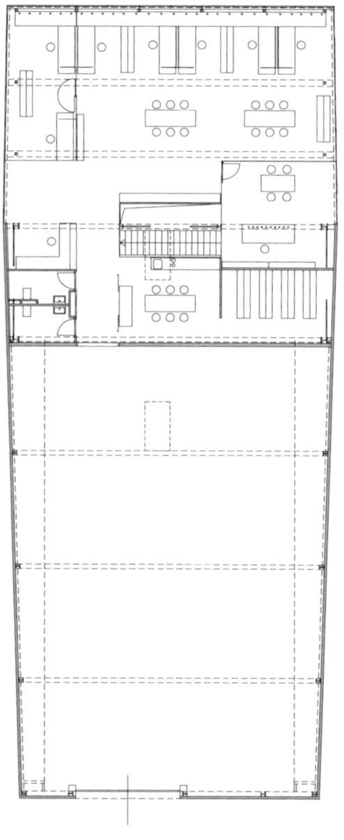

level 1

EFAFLEX

EFAFLEX
warehouse
Baden
2010

The existing plant required a warehouse. In keeping with a master plan, the first step involved erecting a hall measuring 13 × 40 meters positioned adjacent to the delivery bay. The minimized steel construction spanning 11 meters is facilitated by its arched form. On the building's long sides the roof surface stops short of the ground to allow light into the building. The hall is accessible from both ends, easing access to the neutral storage space.

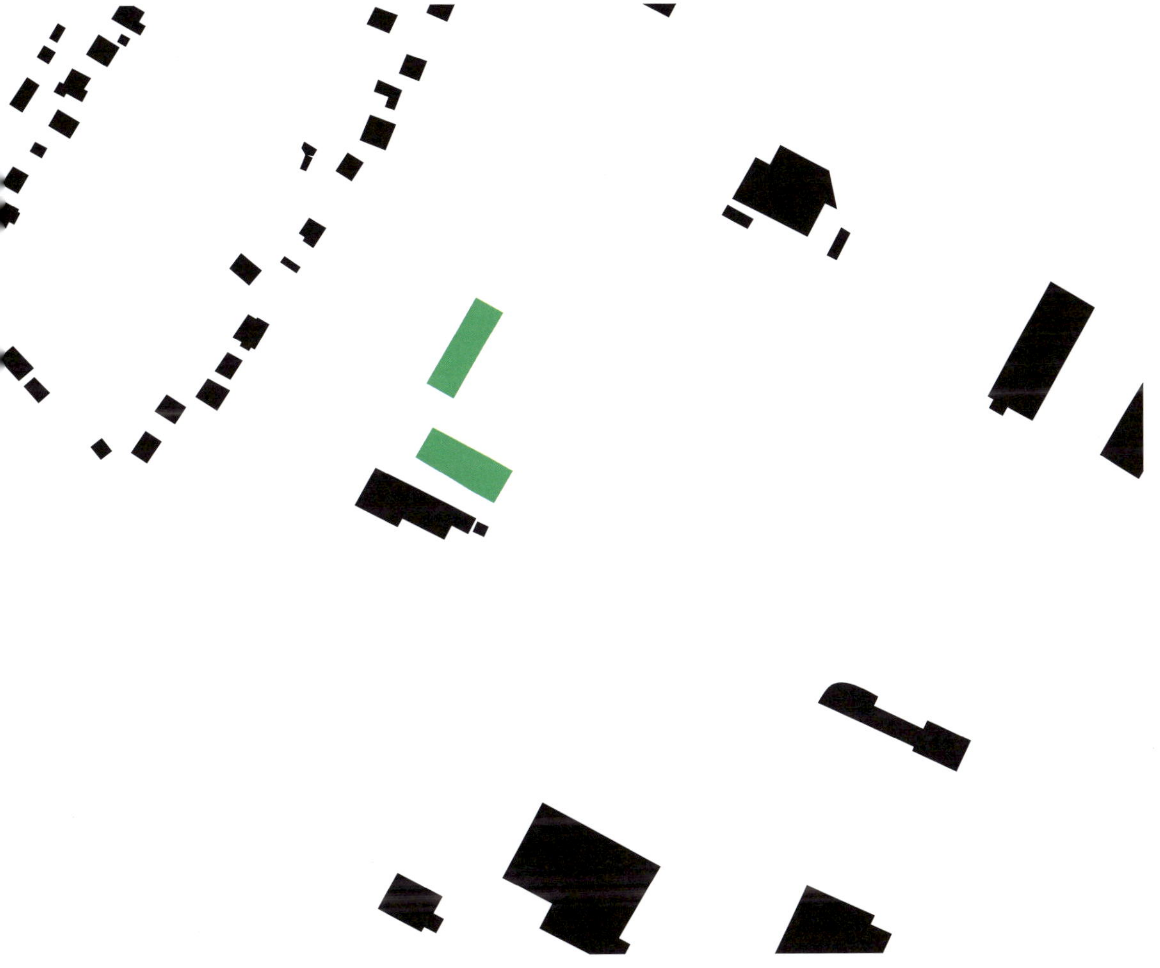

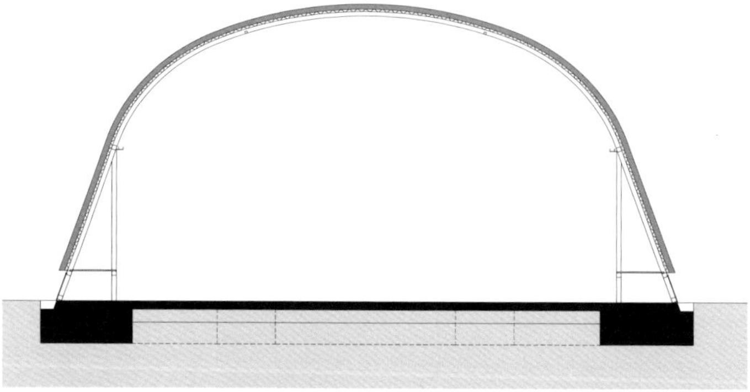

VII Postscript

talking and working

Every now and then, over a cup of coffee or a glass of wine in a café, a bar, or on a building site, the ARTECs tell me about buildings or projects. Richard speaks softly, without inflection, always in the same pitch. Bettina speaks slightly more slowly, a bit louder, and somewhat melodically. Listening requires the utmost concentration, on the one hand, due to the wealth of information, on the other, because the stories sometimes have multiple layers or become intertwined. It is a complex sort of intensity, yet never includes bombardment of the "and-then-I-said-this-and-then-I-did-that" sort – an often encountered pattern – or grumbling about the sorry state of affairs. They are always on-topic. It seems to me that the way they communicate* is a reflection of the work they do together.

names and roots

The era of clever or uptight office names had not yet begun, but Bettina and Richard had to have a programmatic office name. From the very beginning, their aim was to unite art and technology in their work – and to make that unity perceptible. When I close my eyes and think of their buildings, I see aluminum sheet, poplar plywood and a diagonal, orange steel beam, though this particular combination doesn't exist in any of their buildings. I think of an aluminum processing firm in Bludenz named Manahl, and of a subdivision named Halde designed by Hans Purin, also in Bludenz, where Bettina grew up. And of the architecture of Josef Lackner: it was certainly no coincidence that in 2008, when Bettina was Austria's curator to the 11th Venice Architecture Biennale, she took the opportunity to make his work known to an international audience.

brick pile and aluminum cap

I've lost track, but I think this was the first ARTEC project I visited. Perhaps it even prompted me to get in touch with them. That may well have been. In any case, a friendship evolved, as did a continual interest in their work. It is noteworthy and, at the same time, compelling just how often the early work of artists sows seeds, which then put out different shoots and, in some cases, something is later grafted on to it, while the enduring quintessence lies hidden within. Chalk it up to childhood!
I can't imagine a more serendipitous or fitting commission for "ARTEC" than this small building addition for Zita Kern. In an unpretentious, or, better yet, engaging, "messy" farmstead, isolated in the expanse of the Marchfeld, a farmer nurtures her fruit, vegetables, chickens, and

cats. The farmer is also a literary scholar. All she lacked was a space for bathing and another for reading and writing.

The bathroom is on the ground floor, integrated in the existing building near the bedroom: aluminum shimmers and light enters from above. Above it, a clay-toned brick building whose stucco has been removed holds the reading space. Inside, warm poplar plywood, flanked by a wood deck. Outside, from below, along the existing building, a glass-covered stair leads up to the uncontrived, folded cap. The untreated, cold-milled, riveted aluminum sheet isn't perfect, doesn't stay perfect, nor is it intended to be perfect and shimmers, reflecting the sky above the Marchfeld. This shimmering effect, this contrast to duller, more earthy materials, is a recurring theme in ARTEC's buildings.

two figures

I had only seen the EFAFLEX plant in photos. The building massing hoists itself forward and gazes off into the distance on the outskirts of Vienna, near the highway – that's how I'd imagined it. I often came across the image of this pleasant "onlooker," but it wasn't until I saw the photo of the dark, neighboring archway structure that I visited the grounds. The compound is located outside Baden – with its back to the highway, which turns out to be farther off than expected – in an industrial park that is still rather sparsely built.

In Alto Adige there are a number of old farmsteads consisting of a low-slung, shingled, stonemasonry building standing next to a large, lofty wood structure with a steep thatched roof. The demands made of these two buildings were thus probably more complex than the standard solutions in which roof forms are determined by potential precipitation and the roofing materials.

In Baden, a factory hall with elevated offices encounters a cost-efficient warehouse, the latter with no thermal requirements whatsoever. This was not a matter of a quest for formal resonance, instead the structures were developed from the internal demands. One shimmers gently and metallically and reflects the offices' orange tone out into the landscape. Next to it, soft and black, is the serene warehouse, covered in a rubber membrane. The massing of the two structures benefits from a subtle, slight deviation from the strict geometric floor plan and section.

residence for the elderly: a breath of fresh air

Residential towers dating to the nineteen sixties line a broad path, but have no direct relationship to it – to call it a promenade would definitely be going too far. Mature trees impede a direct connection to the river. Suddenly a shimmering building appears, hoisted up seven meters in the air – its elevated underside in a warm shade of yellow. Above the path, it extends almost to the river. Not a heavy lid, but a light ribbon in the air. No longer a "green hell," but rather an urban space with a café and a small chapel on the gently modelled, generously dimensioned ground – children play here, running every which way. The "old folks" live above on long, bright corridors, and the huge roof terraces afford views of the mountains. Chances are good that with the passage of time, the roof terraces will become slightly overgrown and a kebab stand will set up shop down on the square. A miracle is unfolding in the Olympic Village!

a wish of mine: an ARTEC-planned neighborhood

ARTEC realized a precise, airy housing concept in St. Pölten. Based on a concept making use of prefabricated components consisting of concrete columns and reinforced-concrete hollow core slabs, halls measuring roughly 75 by 16 meters are stacked one atop the other. They are fitted out with prefabricated wood components. One side is flanked with the circulation zone, which provides space for informal interaction just outside one's unit, and the other side has a layer accommodating the private outdoor spaces. Numerous floor-plan variations are conceivable, without requiring jumping through hoops. Indeed, Jean Nouvel's apartment building in Nimes, which has a similar concept, is somehow better looking. But with this housing complex, ARTEC developed a type in economically optimized form that anyone can use. It could, for instance, be used to build a "simple" development interwoven with public facilities: variety within a strong framework. I know of no contribution more integral to "housing". And – such thoughts do not arise regarding Nouvel – their concept is not merely a one-off, but could be employed for an entire city!

* There are "other" ways of telling – for example, "role allocation" – which, however, usually don't allow the listener to draw conclusions about how a team works together.

Bettina Götz
born on August 21, 1962, in Bludenz, Austria
1980–87 studied architecture at the Technische Universität in Graz
2005 City of Vienna Architecture Award
since 2006 full professor at the department Entwerfen und Baukonstruktion (Design and Building Technology) at the Universität der Künste in Berlin
2008 curator of the Austrian contribution to the 11th Venice Biennale of Architecture
2015 guest professor at the Università Iuav di Venezia
since 2004 active on advisory boards and commssions in Austria and abroad

Richard Manahl
born on August 23, 1955, in Bludenz, Austria
1973–82 studied architecture at the Technische Universität in Graz
1983–84 worked in the office of Helmut Richter and Heidulf Gerngross
1988–1996 board member of the Österreichischen Gesellschaft für Architektur
2005 City of Vienna Architecture Award
2015 guest professor at the Università Iuav di Venezia
2017 guest professor at ENSA Paris – Val de Seine

Atelier in Vienna since 1985, with Theo Lang from 1985–1992, with Ed Hoke from 1987–1989

Current employees
Gerda Polig, Björn Wilfinger,
Gül Cakar, Héctor Farré Cortada, Johannes Giselbrecht, Karin Haupt, Josef Schröck, Jun Wook Song

Former employees
Andreas Baumgartner, Heinrich Büchel, Irene Carlés Gaspar, Sandra Crisafulli, Jakub Dalek, Verena Eder, Nina Fessler, Marie-Theres Holler, Michael Ivancsics, Maria Kirchweger, Andrea Kopp, Katharina Kothmiller, Bernadette Krejs, Helmut Lackner, Stephan Lechner, Rene Lentsch, Steuart Mackenzie-Harrison, Eva Mair, Lisa Mayr, Ronald Mikolics, Michael Murauer, Judith-Caroline Mussel, Panajota Panotopoulou, Emmanuel Parkmann, Markus Pfändler, Laura Pleifer, Irene Prieler, Lena Schacherer, Burkhard Schelischansky, Vanessa Url, Michael Werner, Michael Wimberger, Anna-Maria Wolf, Irene Yerro, Ivan Zdenkovic, Martin Zechner

All buildings and a selection of lectures, exhibitions and prizes 1984–2017:

1984
Exhibition *Bar jeder Architektur* (Bettina Götz, Theo Lang, Richard Manahl, Stefan Nessmann, Anna Popelka): Harter Laubfrosch, installation for Steirische Herbst, Schlossberg / Graz (Sokratis Dimitriou, curator)

1985
Office on Rüdigergasse, Vienna

1989
Lecture Österreichische Gesellschaft für Architektur (Austrian Society for Architecture), Vienna
Andreas Manahl Residence in Nüziders

1990
Lecture Zentralvereinigung der Architekten Österreichs, Salvatorgasse, Vienna

1992
Lecture *Der Apparat der Formfindung*, Österreichischen Gesellschaft für Architektur, Vienna

1993
Exhibition *Fenster zum Westen*, exhibition display case at the Kunsthalle on Karlsplatz, Vienna (Tony Stooss, curator)
Exhibition *Minimalausstellung*, Department of Residential *Architecture*, TU Wien (Jan Turnovský, curator)
Exhibition participation *Architektur*, Galerie Max Hetzler and Galerie Philomene Magers, Cologne
Exhibition participation *Architektur als Engagement*, Haus der Architektur, Graz (Peter Zinganel, curator)
Exhibition participation *SOS Aufbau Wohnen. Ideen für ein neues soziales Bauen*, Secession, Vienna
Exhibition and lecture *Form folgt dem Wollen und dem Können*, Galerie Walcheturm, Zürich (Eva Presenhuber, curator)
Exhibition architecture *Der zerbrochene Spiegel*, Museumsquartier and Kunsthalle Wien, Wiener Festwochen, Vienna
Office building in Bludenz, Heinrich Manahl GmbH, Bludenz
Residence in Peuerbach

1994
Exhibition *Architektur zeigen. Österreichweite Ausstellung von Architekturobjekten im Original* (Walter Zschokke, curator)
Exhibition *Der Raum der Ausstellung*, Kunst Raum Wien, Museumsquartier, Vienna
Kunstraum Wien, Museumsquartier, Vienna
Lecture Forum Stadtpark, Graz
Courtroom in Leoben,
Styrian Government, Graz
Kunstraum Wien, Markus Brüderlin, curator of the Federal Chancellery, Vienna
Rowhouses on Weiherweg, Nüziders
Spuller Residence, Vienna

1995
Exhibition *ARTEC Wien*, Galerie Aedes, Berlin
Rowhouse complex on Fliederweg, Wolfurt
Exhibition *Plan / Modell / Foto*, Architekturforum Tirol, Innsbruck, 1995; Architekturforum Oberösterreich, Linz; Kunsthaus Bregenz at Galerie Liesi Hämmerle, 1996 (Arno Ritter, curator)
Rowhouses on Fliederweg, Wolfurt

1996
Lecture Bauhaus Universität Weimar
Burgenländische Landesgalerie (Gallery of the Province of Burgenland) in Eisenstadt, in Esterhazy Palace's former stables, sliding wall system
School on Zehdengasse, Kallco-Projekt and City Administration of Vienna

1997
Depot, Wolfgang Zinggl, curator of the Federal Chancellery, Vienna

1998
Exhibition *Beyond the Minimal*, Architectural Association, London; Art Front Gallery, Hillside Terrace, Tokyo; Katsuike School, Kyoto, 1999 (Peter Allison, curator)
Lecture *Architektur ist die Fortsetzung von Natur mit anderen Mitteln*, Art Front Gallery, Tokyo
Lecture *Zita Kern Space*, Architectural Association, London
Lecture Zentralvereinigung der Architekten Österreichs, 20er Haus – Museum of Contemporary Art, Vienna
Zita Kern Space, Raasdorf
Wagenredergründe Housing, Bärnbach, Köflach Land Settlement Society
Aluminum Architecture Prize for Zita Kern Space

1999
Exhibition participation *Home: the twentieth century house*, Glasgow (Deyan Sudijc and Tulga Beyerle, curators)
Lecture Architektenverein Stavanger
Lecture *"Architektentheater"* (with Tini Bauer, Hermann Czech, Heidulf Gerngross, Georg Poduschka, Anna Popelka and Ferdinand Schmatz): at Ars Hungarica Art Center, Budapest, and in the Alte Schmiede, Vienna
Lecture *Wenn das Ziel Architektur heißt, ist das Ergebnis Plastik*, Technical University Zagreb
Kreuz-Apotheke (pharmacy), Peuerbach, Dr. Friedrich Juffmann, Peuerbach
Clients' Prize awarded by the Zentralvereinigung der Architekten to Zita Kern

2000
Lecture *Die einfache Form des Komplexen*, Technical University Munich
Lecture NJIT – New Jersey Institute of Technology, Newark
Lecture *The Simple Form of the Complex*, Gerald D. Hines College, University of Houston
Lecture University of Buffalo, School of Architecture + Planning
Lecture *Vorarlberg Graz Vienna*, Hogeschool vor de Kunsten, Academie van Boukunst, Amsterdam

2001
Lecture *Parallele zur Natur*, Technische Universität zu Braunschweig
Apartment building on Laxenburgerstraße, Vienna, Heimbau and GSG, Vienna

2002
Higher Regional Court in Graz, built-in furniture, Styrian Government, Graz

2003
Lecture *Große Strukturen – Kleine Universen*, Fachhochschule Kiel, Eckernförde
Apotheke zum Löwen von Aspern (pharmacy), Vienna, Dr. Wilhelm Schlagintweit KG / PHOENIX Arzneiwaren GmbH, Vienna
Hochwuhr power station, Felsenau, Feldkirch, Stadtwerke Feldkirch, with Peter Sandbichler
Gym and apartment house on Wiedner Hauptstraße, Mischek Bau AG, Vienna

2004
ARTEC moves to a new office at Hundsturm, Vienna
Exhibition *Rock over Baroque. jung + schön: 7+2*, kunsthaus muerz, Mürzzuschlag, Stmk., 2004;
Galerie Aedes East, Berlin, 2005;
Venice Biennale, 2006 (idea and concept: Wolf D. Prix and Reiner Zettl)
Lecture *Folgt Form Material?* Akademie der bildenden Künste Wien, Vienna
EFAFLEX plant, Baden, Ferdinand Türtscher / EFAFLEX, Baden
Apartment building on Alxingergasse, Vienna, GPA, Vienna
Residential and commercial building on Scheffelstraße, Robert Manahl, Bregenz
Hundsturm (apartment building with office space), Vienna, Mischek Bau AG, Vienna
Clients' Prize awarded by the Zentralvereinigung der Architekten to Dr. W. Schlagintweit / Phoenix Arzneiwaren for the pharmacy in Aspern

2005
Exhibition participation, *a_schau. part three. Austrian architecture of the 20th and 21st centuries*, AzW, Vienna (Gabriele Kaiser and Monika Platzer, curators)
Lecture *Days of ORIS*, Zagreb
Lecture Universität der Künste, Berlin
B-B Residence, Bocksdorf, Burgenland, Austria
S Residence, Bocksdorf, Burgenland, Austria
Rüdigersteg, footbridge, Ernst Arnold Park, Vienna, City Administration of Vienna
Architecture Prize of Austria's Concrete and Cement Industry, for the pharmacy in Aspern
Mies van der Rohe Award, nomination, pharmacy in Aspern
Mies van der Rohe Award, EFAFLEX, one of the "Selected Works"
City of Vienna Architecture Award

2006
Exhibition *www.gaaleriie.net, internet gallery of contemporary architecture* (Alena Hanzlova, curator), Prague
Exhibition participation *Third International Exhibition of Contemporary Design*, Mexico City
Lecture at 5° Congreso, Mexico City, International Interior Design Association
Lecture Tsinghua University, Beijing
Exhibition architecture *The Unknown Loos: Walter*, AzW, Vienna (Sonja Pisarik, curator)

Villa in the Vienna Woods, renovation, Tullnerbach
Interior architecture for an apartment, Vienna
Architecture Prize of the Province of Burgenland for the B – B Residence and S Residence
European Prize for Urban Public Space, Hochwuhr power station finalist

2007
Exhibition architecture *Im Wirtshaus*, Wien Museum Karlsplatz, Vienna
k 6, high-rise on Kundratstrasse, residential and commercial building, Vienna, with Neumann + Partner, GPA-WBV, Vienna
systemhaus 1 in Lauterach, Christoph Manahl, Bregenz

2008
Exhibition Ockham ist schärfer als Mies, Architektur Galerie Berlin, Berlin
Exhibition participation Sense of Architecture, Architektur Laboratorium Steiermark, exhibition with films by Heinz Emigholz, Venice Biennale (among other venues) (Charlotte Pöchhacker and Alexander Kada, curators)
Reiners Stiftung Architecture Prize (private foundation), special prize for the B–B Residence
Burgenland Prize of the Wood Industry for the B–B Residence

2009
Exhibition participation Second Biennial of the Canary Islands: *Parasite Architecture*, Santa Cruz de Tenerife, (Sara Marini, curator)
Lecture *Das Potenzial der "Strasse" als städtebaulichem Strukturelement*, abstract city: streets, UdK Berlin
Lecture *Zita Kern Space*, USI – Accademia di Architettura, Mendrisio
Lecture *Useful Things*, UdK monday, studio arets, public lecture course
EFAFLEX warehouse, Baden, Ferdinand Türtscher / EFAFLEX, Baden
Entrance pavilion SMZ Süd (hospital), Vienna, KAV
Residence in Kefalonia
systemhaus 2 Hörbranz, Christoph and Mira Manahl
Apartment building on Schliemanngasse, Vienna, Bauhilfe
Apartment building on Tokiostrasse, The Town Musicians of Bremen, Vienna, Neues Leben

2010
Lecture *Die Organäisten, Was bleibt von der Grazer Schule?*, IAKK, TU Graz
Lecture *Proto-typische Gewöhnlichkeiten*, Staatliche Akademie der Bildenden Künste, Stuttgart
Lecture *urbanes hausen*, Aedes Network Campus, Berlin
Lecture *Wie Sachen zustande kommen*, afo – architekturforum oberösterreich, Linz
Clients' Prize awarded by the Zentralvereinigung der Architekten to Neues Leben for the apartment building on Tokiostrasse
Mies van der Rohe Award, nomination Tokiostrasse

2011
generationen wohnen am mühlgrund (housing complex), Vienna, BUWOG
Volksgarten discotheque, renovation, with BEHF Architekten, Vienna, Peter Böhm

2012
Apartment building on Raxstrasse, Vienna, win4wien

2013
Lecture *Ockham ist schärfer als Mies*, RTWK Leipzig

2014
Exhibition participation *DETAIL, architecture seen in section*, Venice Biennale (among other venues), (Marco Pogacnik, curator)
Lecture *Das Prinzip des Unfertigen*, symposium, architecture school, UdK Berlin
Lecture *Die gemischte Stadt. Wohnen für alle in Hamburg*, housing conference, Hamburg
Lecture *Living in Vienna*, Forum + Institute for Urban Design, ACFNY, New York
Lecture *Szenisches Architekturgespräch*, formerly *Architektentheater*, OFROOM, adapted from a manuscript by and under the direction of Ferdinand Schmatz with Isabel Walter, and with the architects Hermann Czech, Heidulf Gerngross, Richard Manahl, Anna Popelka, and Georg Poduschka, Vienna
Lecture *Wiener Wohnen*, Architekturtage München
Lecture *Zukunftsfähigkeit beginnt in der Gegenwart*, aut. architektur und tirol, Innsbruck

2015

Exhibition participation *DAHEIM – Bauen und Wohnen in Gemeinschaft*, DAM, Frankfurt, (Annette Becker and Laura Kienbaum, curators)

Lecture *Die Struktur des Unfertigen*, TU Wien, Vienna

Lecture *Aspects and Methods Noticed in our Appreciation of Architecture*, Iuav, Venice

Residence in the Olympic Village, Innsbruck, stadtBAU and ISD

Clients' Prize awarded by the Zentralvereinigung der Architekten to the City of Innsbruck, stadtBau and ISD for the Residence in the Olympic Village

2016

Lecture *Building by Concepts*, ORIS House of Architecture, Zagreb

Lecture *Gründe haben*, Festwochen Gmunden

Volksgarten discotheque, various renovation projects, Vienna, Peter Böhm

Interior architecture for an apartment, Vienna, Eva Presenhuber

Berlin Award 2016 – Heimat in der Fremde, for Maximilianstrasse St. Pölten, with SMAQ

2017

Maria Lassnig's atelier, conversion to depot and exhibition space, Vienna, Maria Lassnig Privatstiftung

Stadtbar, Vienna, Kaveh Ahi Bar

Apartment building on Fritz-Kandl-Gasse, Vienna, GPA-WBV

Apartment building on Fritz-Kandl-Gasse, Vienna, SÜBA

In der Wiesen apartment complex, Vienna, Heimbau / Altmannsdorf und Hetzendorf

Apartment building on Maximilianstrasse, St. Pölten, BWSG

Housing on Saalachstrasse, Salzburg, Heimat Österreich

2018

Grangasse, attic addition, Vienna, Neuraum und Heindl Leasing

Apartment building on Bergmannstraße, Bregenz, Christoph Manahl

Harter Laubfrosch (Tough Frog)
installation on Graz's Schlossberg
Steirischer Herbst, Graz, 1984
"Bar jeder Architektur"
team: Bettina Götz, Theo Lang, Richard Manahl, Stefan Nessmann, Anna Popelka
→ 161–165

administrative offices of building authority
competition, first prize, unrealized
Graz, 1988
team: Bettina Götz, Ed Hoke, Theo Lang, Richard Manahl
→ 22

Europan 1
competition, Graz, 1989
team: Bettina Götz, Theo Lang, Richard Manahl
→ 20

Essling, Europan 2
competition, Vienna, 1991
team: Bettina Götz, Theo Lang, Richard Manahl
→ 14

vocational school, addition
competition, Bregenz, 1991
team: Bettina Götz, Theo Lang, Richard Manahl
→ 26

3 s, exhibition project
SOS Aufbau Wohnen, Vienna, 1993
team: Bettina Götz, Richard Manahl, Martin Zechner
→ 10–11

Fuzzy House
Galerie Max Hetzler and Galerie Philomene Magers, Cologne, 1993
team: Bettina Götz, Richard Manahl
→ 7–9, 67

The Broken Mirror
Museumsquartier, Messepalast Hall B
Kunsthalle, Wiener Festwochen, Vienna, 1993 (May 26 – July 25, 1993)
Kasper König and Hans-Ulrich Obrist, curators, team: Bettina Götz, Richard Manahl
→ 166

Sand housing complex
competition, Lustenau, 1993
team: Bettina Götz, Theo Lang, Richard Manahl
→ 12–13

nursing school, addition
competition, Graz, 1993
team: Bettina Götz, Richard Manahl, Martin Zechner
→ 24

Spuller Residence
Vienna, 1994
team: Bettina Götz, Theo Lang, Richard Manahl
→ 16

Kunstraum
Fischer Wing, Museumsquartier,
Markus Brüderlin, curator of the Federal Chancellery, Vienna, 1994
team: Bettina Götz, Richard Manahl
→ 92

Prado Museum, addition
competition, Madrid, 1995
team: Bettina Götz, Marie-Therese Holler, Maria Kirchweger, Richard Manahl, Martin Zechner
→ 28

school on Zehdengasse
Kallco-Projekt and City Administration of Vienna, Vienna, 1996
team: Verena Eder, Bettina Götz, Marie-Theres Holler, Maria Kirchweger, Richard Manahl, Steuart Mackenzie-Harrison, Judith-Karoline Mussel, Markus Pfändler, Christian Seidl, Martin Zechner
→ 214–215

eine Stadtstruktur (an urban framework)
City of Vienna, Vienna, 1996
team: Bettina Götz, Richard Manahl
→ 18, 36

Depot
Fischer Wing, Museumsquartier
Wolfgang Zinggl, curator of the Federal Chancellery, Vienna, 1997
team: Bettina Götz, Richard Manahl
→ 93

Bad zur Sonne
competition, Graz, 1997
team: Bettina Götz, Richard Manahl
→ 108

Costantini Museum
competition, Buenos Aires, 1997
team: Bettina Götz, Richard Manahl
→ 106

Zita Kern Space
Zita Kern, Raasdorf, 1998
team: Bettina Götz, Maria Kirchweger, Richard Manahl
→ 130–139

urn field
competition, Linz, 1999
team: Bettina Götz, Richard Manahl
→ 167

apartment building on Laxenburgerstrasse
Heimbau and GSG Wien, Vienna, 2001
team: Bettina Götz, Marie-Theres Holler, Maria Kirchweger, Richard Manahl, Ivan Zdenkovic
→ 44

apartment building and gym on Hollgasse
Mischek Bau AG, Vienna, 2003
city planning concept with Lainer + Partner and s&s architekten
team: Marie-Therese Holler, Maria Kirchweger, Bettina Götz, Richard Manahl, Michael Werner, Ivan Zdenkovic
→ 128–129

pharmacy “Zum Löwen von Aspern”
Dr. Wilhelm Schlagintweit KG and Phoenix Arnzneiwaren GmbH, Vienna, 2003
with Oskar Graf Engineers
team: Bettina Götz, Richard Manahl, Ronald Mikolics, Irene Prieler
→ 46, 200–211

EFAFLEX plant
Ferdinand Türtscher / EFAFLEX, Baden, 2004
team: Bettina Götz, Richard Manahl, Irene Prieler
→ 226–233

apartment building on Alxingergasse
GPA-WBV, Vienna, 2004
team: Bettina Götz, Marie-Theres Holler, Maria Kirchweger, Richard Manahl, Ronald Mikolics, Michael Werner
→ 172

Am Hundsturm – apartment building with office space
Mischek Bau AG, Vienna, 2004
team: Marie-Theres Holler, Bettina Götz, Maria Kirchweger, Richard Manahl, Ronald Mikolics, Irene Prieler, Michael Werner
→ 174

B–B Residence
Bocksdorf, 2005
team: Bettina Götz, Helmut Lackner, Richard Manahl, Ronald Mikolics
→ 78–85

S Residence
Bocksdorf, 2005
team: Bettina Götz, Helmut Lackner, Richard Manahl, Ronald Mikolics
→ 86

swimming pools in Schruns-Tschagguns
competition, Tschagguns, 2006
team: Bettina Götz, Richard Manahl, Ronald Mikolics, Panajota Panotopoulou, Ivan Zdenkovic
→ 96

K 6, high-rise on Kundratstrasse
GPA-WBV, Vienna, 2007
with Neumann + Partner
team: Bettina Götz, Helmut Lackner, Richard Manahl, Ronald Mikolics, Michael Werner, Anna-Maria Wolf
→ 212–213

headquarters, Salewa International
competition, Bolzano, 2007
team: Nina Fessler, Bettina Götz, Richard Manahl, Panajota Panotopoulou, Anna-Maria Wolf
→ 110

Skanstes Street
competition, Riga, 2007
team: Nina Fessler, Bettina Götz, Richard Manahl, Ronald Mikolics, Panajota Panotopoulou, Irene Yerro
→ 168

apartment building on Tokiostrasse, The Town Musicians of Bremen
Neues Leben, Vienna, 2009
team: Heinrich Büchel, Bettina Götz, Michael Ivancsics, Richard Manahl, Ronald Mikolics, Michael Murauer, Irene Yerro
→ 42–43, 142–154

hospital entrance pavilion, SMZ Süd
KAV, Wiener Krankenanstaltenverbund, Vienna, 2009
team: Bettina Götz, Bernadette Krejs, Richard Manahl, Ronald Mikolics, Michael Murauer
→ 218–225

systemhaus 2
Christoph and Mira Manahl, Hörbranz, 2009
team: Johannes Giselbrecht, Bettina Götz, Gerda Polig, Richard Manahl, Michael Murauer
→ 68–77

Spark, feasibility study
Grunt a.s. Bratislava, 2009
team: Bettina Götz, Richard Manahl, Michael Murauer, Anna-Maria Wolf
→ 38, 170–171

EFAFLEX warehouse
Ferdinand Türtscher / EFAFLEX, Baden, 2010
team: Johannes Giselbrecht, Bettina Götz, Richard Manahl, Anna-Maria Wolf
→ 234–238

pre-school in Stadtpark
competition, Vienna, 2010
team: Bettina Götz, Richard Manahl, Michael Murauer, Gerda Polig
→ 216

multi-generational housing: at Mühlweg
BUWOG, Vienna, 2011
team: Bettina Götz, Richard Manahl, Ronald Mikolics, Michael Murauer, Björn Wilfinger, Anna-Maria Wolf
→ 47, 182–192

public library, Daegu Gosan
Competition, Daegu Gosan, 2012
team: Bettina Götz, Richard Manahl, Jun Wook Song
→ 180–181

school campus in Gnigl
competition, Salzburg, 2013
team: Gül Cakar, Bettina Götz, Richard Manahl, Gerda Polig, Jun Wook Song
→ 178–179

apartment building on Raxstrasse
win4wien + Gesellschafter, Vienna, 2012
city planning concept with Architect Krischanitz and Lainer + Partner
team: Heinrich Büchel, Johannes Giselbrecht, Bettina Götz, Richard Manahl, Ronald Mikolics, Michael Murauer, Gerda Polig
→ 48–60

residence in the Olympic Village
stadtBAU Innsbruck and ISD, Innsbruck, 2015
team: Bettina Götz, Eva Mair, Richard Manahl, Gerda Polig, Josef Schröck, Jun Wook Song, Björn Wilfinger
→ 112–127

interior architecture / Eva Presenhuber
Vienna, 2016
team: Bettina Götz, Irene Carlés Gaspar, Richard Manahl, Jun Wook Song
→ 90

apartment building on Fritz-Kandl-Gasse
SÜBA, Vienna, 2017
team: Gül Cakar, Bettina Götz, Stephan Lechner, Richard Manahl, Lisa Mayr, Jun Wook Song, Björn Wilfinger
→ 98

apartment building on Fritz-Kandl-Gasse
GPA, Vienna, 2017
team: Gül Cakar, Irene Carlés Gaspar, Bettina Götz, Stephan Lechner, Richard Manahl, Lisa Mayr, Jun Wook Song, Björn Wilfinger
→ 98

housing on Saalachstrasse
Heimat Österreich, Salzburg, 2017
team: Irene Carlés Gaspar, Bettina Götz, Stephan Lechner, Richard Manahl, Gerda Polig, Jun Wook Song
→ 176

In der Wiesen housing complex
Altmannsdorf Hetzendorf and Heimbau, Vienna, 2017
city planning concept with Dietrich I Untertrifaller Architekten
team: Gül Cakar, Bettina Götz, Stephan Lechner, Richard Manahl, Emmanuel Parkmann, Gerda Polig, Josef Schröck, Jun Wook Song, Björn Wilfinger
→ 40

apartment building on Maximilianstrasse
BWSG, St. Pölten, 2017
with wup wimmerundpartner and raum & kommunikation (SMAQ)
team: Gül Cakar, Héctor Farré Cortada, Johannes Giselbrecht, Bettina Götz, Richard Manahl, Josef Schröck, Jun Wook Song
→ 88

Atelier Maria Lassnig, conversion to depot and exhibition space
Maria Lassnig Foundation, Vienna, 2017
team: Bettina Götz, Richard Manahl, Gerda Polig
→ 94–95

apartment building on Bergmannstrasse, renovation and addition
Christoph Manahl, Bregenz, 2018
team: Bettina Götz, Richard Manahl, Elisabeth Mayr, Gerda Polig
→ 140

Grangasse attic conversion
Neuraum R/H GmbH, Vienna, 2018
team: Bettina Götz, Richard Manahl, Josef Schröck, Jun Wook Song
→ 141

Das Haus der Zukunft – IBA reloaded? Abstract City 17
edited by Bettina Götz. Verlag der Universität der Künste, Berlin 2017

Wie Weiterbauen? Abstract City 07
edited by Bettina Götz. Verlag der Universität der Künste, Berlin 2012

Urbanes Hausen. Abstract City 04
edited by Bettina Götz. Verlag der Universität der Künste, Berlin 2010

Building Education. Abstract City 02
edited by Bettina Götz. Verlag der Universität der Künste, Berlin 2010

Strassen. Abstract City 01
edited by Bettina Götz. Verlag der Universität der Künste, Berlin 2009

Before Architecture. Vor der Architektur.
11th International Architecture Exhibition – La Biennale di Venezia
edited by Bettina Götz. Springer Publishing, Vienna/NY 2008

ARTEC Architekten. Catalogue for the internet exhibition project by Alena Hanzlova (editor), Prague, 2006

Beyond The Minimal. Peter Allison (curator)
book accompanying the exhibition
AA, London 1998

Projekte 1994 – 1996
edited by Kunstraum Wien
Triton, Vienna 1996

ARTEC Wien. Bürogebäude in Bludenz, Volksschule in Wien
exhibition catalog, Aedes West
Berlin 1995

ARTEC. Plan Modell Foto
exhibition catalog, Architekturforum Tirol
Innsbruck 1995

ARTEC Architekten, Arbeiten bis 1994
exhibition catalog, Kunst Raum Wien
Museumsquartier, Vienna 1994

Photography

ARTEC Architekten
3/4, 7, 9, 14, 22, 36, 40, 47, 63/64, 81, 84, 85, 86, 93, 96, 98, 101/102, 108, 110, 130, 133, 140, 141, 148, 150, 157/158, 161, 162/163, 164/165, 168, 170, 178, 180, 186/187, 188, 195/196, 217, 234, 237, 238, 241/242

Damil Kalogjera (Oris)
244

Paul Giuliani
16

Herta Hurnaus
129

Bruno Klomfar
53, 54, 58/59, 60, 71, 72, 73, 74, 75, 76, 77, 90, 119, 122/123, 124, 189, 191

Florian Kloss
13

Karl Krauss
92

Paul Ott
44, 82/83, 84, 86

Andreas Praefcke
31/32

Lukas Schaller
55, 56, 57, 95, 116, 117, 118, 120, 121, 125, 126, 127, 174, 190, 192, 213

Sylvia Schlagintweit
207

Herbert Schwingenschlögl
167

Margherita Spiluttini, © Architekturzentrum Wien, Sammlung
42, 43, 46, 134/135, 136, 137, 138, 139, 147, 149, 151, 152, 153, 154, 172, 204, 205, 206, 208/209, 210, 211, 222, 223, 224/225, 226, 229, 230, 231, 232/233, 244

Rupert Steiner
214, 215

Gerald Zugmann
10, 18, 24, 26, 28, 106, 212

Book concept:
Bettina Götz, Richard Manahl,
Arno Ritter

Text editing: Arno Ritter
Translation and proofreading:
Elise Feiersinger

Book design: grafisches Büro
Image editing: pixelstorm
Paper: Munken Lynx 120g, Fancy Emboss
Printing: Holzhausen

Park Books AG
Niederdorfstrasse 54
8001 Zürich
Switzerland
www.park-books.com

Park Books is being supported by the Federal Office of Culture with a general subsidy for the years 2016–2020.

Printed on paper certified by the FSC and produced in keeping with the Austrian ecolabel.

ISBN 978-3-03860-092-3